The Foreigners Are in 709

An American Family Livin' the Life in China

May 2012- July 2013

Hope Solomon Young

Copyright © 2018 by Hope Solomon Young

All rights reserved. With the exception of short quotations for articles and reviews, no part of this publication may be reproduced, transmitted, scanned, distributed, stored in any form or by any means, electronic, mechanical, photocopying, recording, or otherwise, without prior written permission from the author.

Cover art and design by Ella Young.
Author photograph by Glenn Nash.

Published in the United States of America by

FLOATING LEAF PRESS

A division of
WordPlay
Maureen Ryan Griffin
6420 A-1 Rea Road, Suite 218,
Charlotte, NC 28277
Email: info@wordplaynow.com
www.wordplaynow.com

ISBN 978-0-9802304-9-9

to Jim, Rose, and Ella

Table of Contents

Preface 7
Disclaimer 8
Itinerary and Maps 9
About Us 13
    Who We Are 13
    Why and Where We Go 15
    How We Do It 19
Touring China 25
    Hong Kong 25
    Shenzhen 30
    Guangzhou 33
    Sanya 36
    Guangzhou and Ella's Orphanage 48
    Shanghai 53
    Hangzhou and High-Speed Trains 63
    Nanjing 73
    Hefei and Rose's Orphanage 77
    Arriving in Beijing 85
Settling into Beijing, July 7 - August 9 88
    School 88
    Apartment Hunting and Making A Home 93
    Identity Crisis 113
    Setting Up the Household 117
    Taoranting Park, Beijing Zoo, and The Flood 123
    Rose's 11th Birthday and The Summer Palace 130
    Restaurants and Food 132
    Check Out This Menu 141
First Visa Trip: Taiwan 144
Exploring and Making a Life in Beijing,
                August 13 – October 13 154
    Famous Beijing Sights 154
    Yes, The Young Family Adopts Another Girl 160
    Friends 164

Searching for The Perfect Massage	175
Second Visa Trip: Trying to Get to Mongolia	179
Everyday Life in Beijing, October 14 – December 11	184
Traffic, The Getup, Brooms, Dusters, Crowds, Pictures, Ready for Winter	184
How I See Life in China	191
Our Daily Life	195
Our Neighborhood	197
Heat	203
Thanksgiving in China	205
Teaching	207
Third Visa Trip: Bangkok, Thailand— What A Great Place	214
Fourth Visa Trip: Did I Tell You We Love Thailand?	218
Fifth Visa Trip: Who Knew South Korea Was So Great?	234
Travel in China: Jiangsu Province with Jenny	243
Sixth Visa Trip: We Like Japan, But …	248
Marathon to Know Everything Beijing, May 4 – July 1	276
Mutianyu (The Great Wall of China)	276
Family Weekend Excursions	284
Mother's Day Weekend—TRB and Zhongshan Park	286
Pizza Hut, Prince Gongs Mansion, and More	295
Travel in China: Yunnan Province	308
Making Our Way Back to America	331
Unwanted Staycation	331
Coming Home	337
Afterword	343
Hindsight	343
Travel Tips	345
Acknowledgments	347

Preface

During our year in China, I found I really enjoyed writing our travel blog. Not to brag, but I get some positive feedback AND people actually read it—I test them and can tell they did actually read it. Since we've come home, I've shared our stories and pictures—with people who ask—and I keep being told, "You should write a book." Maybe they just wanted me to stop talking? Too bad because now I'm turning my blog into a book.

First and foremost, "The book" is for my children and, I hope someday, grandchildren. My wish is that it serves to preserve the memories of what our family did from May 31, 2012, until our return to the U.S. on July 15, 2013. I hope this book might also help those who want to know what it's like to live overseas or who want to try it themselves. I also hope it gives you a glimpse of what life in China is like today.

As you read, feel free to skip around. The first few sections will give you some background on our family and why we made the decisions we did and how we made our plans. Then, I take you from place to place as we travel up the east coast of China. After that, I describe our life and sights in Beijing and our travels to other Asian countries.

I think some of our stories and the things we learn are entertaining. See what you think. In short, sit back, relax, and just enjoy the ride.

Disclaimer

I want to clarify that this was <u>our</u> "big adventure." This is how <u>we</u> saw things through middle-class American eyes based on our background, education, and past experiences.

I think cultural differences are all around us, even from family to family. Back in the day, my best friend, Rhonda, loved to come to my house because we had a wide variety of pickles and sherbets in the fridge that her family didn't eat. I loved her house because there were so many kids, something was always going on, and they had everything for ice cream sundaes … and I mean everything. I also thought it was interesting that her family left the butter out. Ours was always refrigerated.

The first night eating at another friend's house, I ended the meal somewhat formally— "Thank you for the nice meal, Mrs. Hincks. May I please be excused now?" Everyone laughed, including her parents. I was a little embarrassed, but that's what we did at our house. We had a lot of rules, and this family was a little looser.

So, no matter if it's just down the street or halfway around the world, people say, eat, and do things differently. Some of them may even strike you as funny.

All this being said, my wish is that this book alerts you to some of the differences between the U.S. and China, so you're prepared and shows you some of the delights, so you don't miss out. Our time in China was amazing. We hope to inspire others to take their own big adventures.

Itinerary & Maps

June 6 - 11, 2012	Hong Kong
June 11 - 12	Shenzhen
June 12 - 13	Guangzhou
June 13—20	Sanya
June 20 - 24	Guangzhou (Ella's orphanage—Qing Yuan City)
June 24 - 30	Shanghai
June 30 - July 3	Hangzhou
July 3 - 4	Nanjing
July 4 - 7	Hefei (Rose's orphanage—Huainan)
July 7	Beijing - home base
August 9 - 13	Taiwan
September 21- 23	Tianjin
October 13 - 14	Mongolia (Erlian, China)
December 11 - 16	Thailand
Jan 24 - Feb 22	Thailand
	Bangkok (24-8)
	Chiang Mai (8-15)
	Koh Pha Ngan (15-19)
March 20 - 25	South Korea
April 4- 9	Jiangsu Province (Nanjing 7-9)
April 25 - May 4	Japan
	Tokyo (25-29)
	Mt Fuji (29-30)
	Kyoto (30-3)
June 12 - 18	Yunnan Province
	Kunming (12-13)
	Dali (13-15)
	Lijiang (15-17)

The following maps are included for your reference as you read the book and travel with us. The first is a map of China with the cities we visit circled. The other map is of Asia with the countries we visit circled. It might be helpful to put a Post-it to mark these pages for easy access.

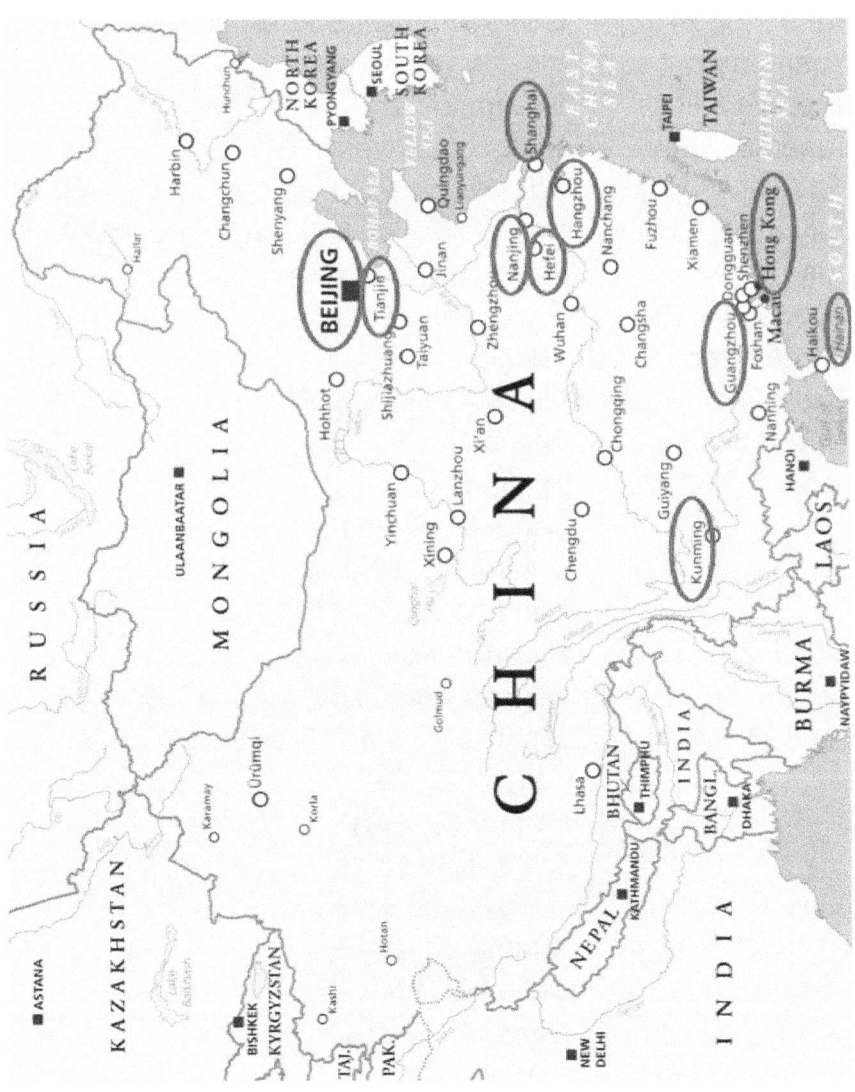

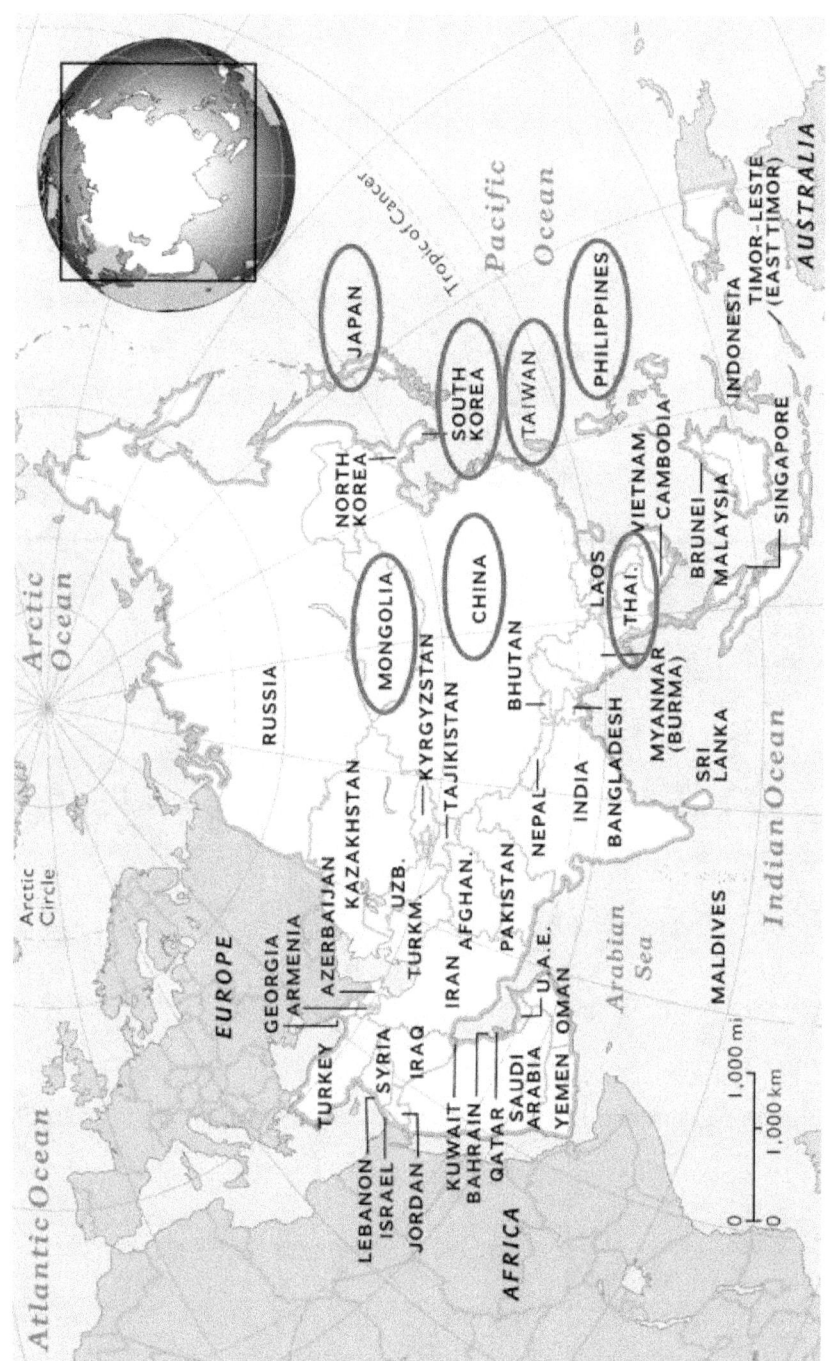

Ella, Hope, Jim and Rose at the interior entrance to the Forbidden City

About Us

Who We Are

So, why did we go to China? What did we do? Where did we go? How did we do it? And, who are we??? Let's start with who we are.

I'm Hope. I grew up in a small town like no other—Hot Springs, Virginia—home of The Homestead Hotel and the largest pumped storage dam in the world. The Homestead was a five-star resort and because of this Hot Springs, during my years there, was a mini UN. People came from all over the world to work and stay there. All this, with a population of less than five thousand people.

I'm a graduate of William and Mary, I'm a marketer (maybe writer), and this adventure started when I was fifteen. In high school, my sister, Eve, hosted an exchange student from Chile. Then, when she didn't complete the exchange, I decided to—twice. The first time to Chile with Open Door, and the second to Spain with The Experiment in International Living.

With the second program, I was awarded a partial scholarship with a requirement of writing a thank-you letter saying what I had learned from the trip. At seventeen, I wrote that I wasn't sure what I had learned. (I couldn't write I now knew what a porron was and could drink wine from it like a native.) I wrote that being exposed to a new culture opened so many avenues that only over time would I realize what this trip truly would mean to me. Well, scholarship people, I now know that these exchange programs taught me to love the world, have the confidence to see it, experience it like a native, and show it to my children. Thank you ... money well spent.

My husband, Jim, is from Oak Ridge, Tennessee. He's a CPA with an MBA and a master's in accounting. He's truly the eternal student with a love of travel and languages. He diligently studied Mandarin for four years in preparation for our trip. Jim owns a small CPA firm that specializes in tax and has some great people who work with him.

Jim did most of the trip planning, including finding and contacting a relocation company to secure a school for the girls and housing for us. He also planned our flights and first six weeks of travel in China. Yay, Jim.

Between the two of us, we've tried to see as much of the world as lives with jobs and families will allow. From age three to six, Jim's family lived in Japan. He spent a college summer in Europe and a winter holiday in Hong Kong. Since college, together and separately, we've traveled in Europe and Central America, and to China for our girls' adoptions.

Our children, Rose and Ella, were both adopted from China at eleven months old, in 2002 and 2003 respectively. Rose is ten when we leave for China and Ella starts the trip at age nine. This is their first trip back to their homeland.

Ella and Rose attended EE Waddell Language Academy in the Chinese immersion program. This is a Charlotte, North

Carolina, public magnet school where the girls learned to speak, write, and read in Mandarin with teachers from Taiwan and mainland China— Ella through third grade and Rose through fourth—before the big adventure begins.

As a family, we have subjected ourselves to other adventures in the past, including a five-week stay in Mexico where the girls and Jim went to Spanish camp. I immersed myself in the culture by shopping. We also endured a sailing time-share experience for six months in which we sailed the coast of South Carolina.

In other words, we tested the "being together a lot in unfamiliar territory" situation before embarking on our China trip. When things in China didn't go as planned, we could always fall back on—well, this isn't as scary as our sailboat almost slamming into the bridge in Shem Creek, or Daddy isn't as sick as he got from eating at that restaurant in Cuernavaca—proving to ourselves that everything in life is relative and through most things, you come out alive.

Why and Where We Go

When we adopted Rose and Ella, part of the paperwork included a form we signed saying we would teach our children about their Chinese heritage. We took this to heart and, you know, any excuse to travel. Given this, we always knew we would at least return to China for the two-week heritage trip, taking the girls back to their orphanages and "finding places."

For those not entrenched in Chinese adoption, China began a one-child policy in 1979 to help control population growth. Males are more valued than females in the Chinese culture since, traditionally, the oldest male child stays with the parents to provide care and money as the parents age. Therefore, most adopted Chinese children are girls who were left by their parents in safe places to be found and taken to a local orphanage. This way, the parents could try again for a boy.

Since Rose and Ella are already in a Chinese immersion program, we like to travel, we want the girls to really learn their language and culture, we have flexible jobs (technology helps with this) and we're a little crazy, the idea of a China trip starts to seriously take shape about a year before we leave. From talking with others and reading, we know we want to visit China before the girls hit their teenage years when they won't want to be seen with us. With the price of airfare and the girls heading toward teenhood soon, the two-week heritage trip grows into "why don't we go for the summer?" which morphs into "Why not stay six months until tax season begins?." Once we settle in China with our one-year leased apartment, convince ourselves the girls can manage school, and realize we'll be homeless in Charlotte since we rented our own home for a year, we decide it's best to stay in China the whole year.

Our itinerary begins with visiting family. From the East coast, we fly to San Francisco to visit Jim's twin brother and family for five days. We have a wonderful visit and find it's a great way to break up the travel and get used to time changes. Plus, Cousin Tommy, thirteen at the time, is a tremendous help. He sets me up with Dropbox to save our pictures to the cloud and we start a blog.

The California crew, all except for Aunt Patty

From San Francisco, we fly to Hong Kong for five days. Our travel for the next four weeks mainly consists of traveling the East coast of China—Shenzhen, Guangzhou, Sanya, Guangzhou (Ella's orphanage tour), Shanghai, Hangzhou, Nanjing, Hefei (Rose's orphanage tour), and Beijing.

Jim plans our itinerary and all our hotel reservations based on our *Lonely Planet* guidebook and Expedia recommendations. I note this because some of our accommodations aren't quite what we expect, and this colors our experiences. Since we've never been to most of these places, it's hard to get it right all the time, especially on a budget. And, yes, we're definitely on a budget. Plus, we want a somewhat authentic Chinese experience. We're not going to China to stay at Holiday Inns and eat at McDonalds the whole trip.

For our home base, Jim knows we need a city where Mandarin is the main language spoken on the street and not a Chinese dialect. We want not only to study the language but also to use it. Beijing fits this criterion. So, based on Mandarin, we decide to live in Beijing.

Just because we have a home base, doesn't mean our traveling days are over. Because we're on Chinese tourist visas, we're required to leave China every sixty days. When we renew our visas in February, the girls and I are required to leave China every thirty days.

When we get the original visas, I think the sixty-day requirement must be something not adhered to because I've never heard of this before. It also doesn't make economic sense to me. Good old American reasoning makes me question why a country would want you to leave and spend your money elsewhere. But, my knowledge is based on being a visitor in foreign countries and not on living there. Many countries have this stipulation.

Having to leave China so frequently does add unexpected expenses to a fairly tight travel budget, but it turns out to be a wonderful gift. Per the visa requirement, we only have to leave China and reenter, but we usually make these exits five-day stays to actually see other countries without interfering too much with the girls' school work. So, we visit Taiwan, Mongolia, Thailand (twice), South Korea, and Japan.

How We Do It

Let' talk money for a minute. I believe our budget was close to $70,000 for the year, but I added another $10,000 for our four-week stay in Thailand and our trip to South Korea. So, although with time it's gotten a little fuzzy and with changing the duration of our stay, I think we spend around $80,000 for our year living in China and our added travel excursions.

A big help with affording the trip is that we left few expenses in the U.S. We rented our house for an amount almost covering all our household expenses. Having our cars paid off and leaving them with friends to use alleviated car payments and storage costs.

Here's how the planning of our trip unfolds. Jim finds a company online, Our Man in Beijing (Richard Collett is our contact and the owner), that agrees to help us find a school for the girls in Beijing and find us housing. Jim pays $2,000 for these services. We later find out Our Man in Beijing usually helps companies and people connect with manufacturers in China and really isn't a relocation company. That said, they do a great job vetting the schools for us and finding out whether the schools will accept the girls on tourist visas.

Our Man in Beijing narrows the school choices down and we choose Beijing Yucai School. The school is two blocks from the Temple of Heaven - one of the top five historic sites in Beijing. Beijing Yucai's brochure boasts that it was founded in 1937 and "is the first school of basic education originated by the Chinese Communist Party." The brochure pictures Mao Zedong with his teacher Xu Teli, who was the first principal of Beijing Yucai. The location in the ancient part of Beijing and the history of the school more than satisfy our need to have our children in an authentic Chinese school.

As you may have guessed, Beijing Yucai is a Chinese public school, not an International or American school. Although Beijing Yucai does have an international component, it's not what you might think. The International Department is composed of students mainly fourteen and older from Mongolia and Korea and teaches them how to read, write and speak Chinese.

We fill out the school applications complete with our girls' school records and a 650 yuan/child fee (just less than $110/child). We are then officially accepted into the Chinese portion of the school although the International Department acts as our liaison. We pay 11,450 yuan/child ($1,908) for the first semester and later 10,000 yuan ($1,666) each for the second semester. This includes tuition, books, lunch, activities, insurance, and uniforms. All of the students in Ella's class except Ella board at the school Monday through Friday. So, that's also an option with an additional charge.

Next, we get permission from EE Waddell to take the girls out of the language program and to have them re-enrolled when we return. The principal and school are extremely supportive and, proudly, they do not only talk the immersion talk but also walk the walk. Everything is made easy for us from taking the girls out of school a week early to having them ride the school bus the first day of the following year.

Then, Jim buys the plane tickets. We apply for our Visas through an online company I wouldn't recommend. We get travel insurance through On Call International ($590 for the family for a year). A Waddell friend, Caroline, recommends them as a good provider, easily accessed online. She also recommends Always and Forever Adoption Homeland Tours to arrange the girls' orphanage visits.

We make doctor visits. In addition, the girls go to Travel Health, a medical practice that specializes in immunizations for foreign travel. Jim and I go to the health department to get shots and medications we can't get from our doctors.

My big contribution to our endeavor is getting our house rented. This means packing up everything and getting someone to pay us for living there. Scott and Maria with the W Realty Group have helped us buy and sell several houses and have become friends as well as business contacts. So, I call them, and they agree to help.

I must say, it's a perfect storm for house rentals. No one is buying houses in this "great recession" because who knows whether you'll have a job next week. If you're lucky enough to sell your house or if you just moved to the Charlotte area, you rent. Also, the Democratic National Convention is coming to Charlotte and everyone's going to make a fortune in the week to two weeks it's here. So, why do a long-term rental when you can rent your home for this abbreviated period and make a bundle? In short, there's nothing nice to rent in Charlotte ... except our house.

Within a month, our house is rented furnished for an amount that pays our mortgage, with the renters paying most of the utilities. We actually could have saved money living in China except for the added costs of our Visa-invoked trips. Our rent in China was a fourth of what our mortgage is. We are also lucky to get great renters who take care of our house. I think we do more damage in the first week we're back with our elderly dog than they did the whole year.

Speaking of our dog, Valentino, our good friend Page takes him in for the duration. Page is a nurturer and Valentino, a fourteen-year-old standard poodle, flourishes under her care. Who wouldn't? She cooks for him, carries him around on his dog bed (he's forty pounds), and talks baby talk to him. He also has two other old dogs to hang out with, and her large back yard is a garden with a pool where Val lounges daily. At Valentino's advanced age, we're a little worried he may not live to see us return. He does, however, and we joke that he thought he died and went to heaven during our absence. Maybe Page's house should be referred to as The Temple of Heaven?

Next, we buy Lonely Planet's guide to China and we pack our bags. We know we're going to be traveling for six weeks before we get to Beijing and need to travel light. I mandate that everyone is allowed five tops, five bottoms, pajamas, toiletries, a pair of sneakers, a pair of sandals and as much underwear as wanted. One small stuffed animal and a "blankie" also make the cut. Our medicines take up an incredible amount of space—more than I ever could have imagined—most of which we never use, including the year's supply of malaria pills.

We pack two small rolling bags, one large rolling duffle, two backpacks and a computer bag. We haven't traveled in a while and don't weigh the bags or pack the liquids correctly. So, we lose some lotion and bug spray and have to pay for an overweight bag. In San Francisco, we borrow a bag from Jim's brother to put the extra weight in. In the end, we have eight bags, including my purse. This is important because we religiously count our bags after loading and unloading them from planes, taxis, hotels, trains, etc. I highly recommend this.

However, the most important thing we take with us is our trip motto— "It's an adventure." This is what we live by. If it is a great experience—it's an adventure. If it's something we don't want to repeat—it's still part of the adventure.

And it worked. I know that because on one hot July afternoon when we'd been living in Beijing for about three weeks, I wanted to take a new route to Wal-Mart to show the girls the hutong (an old neighborhood connected by alleyways) near our apartment. I take a wrong turn and by the time I realize, it's too late to turn back. So, we walk over several fields of ugly construction rubble, including broken glass and other sharp objects, in our flip flops, in the blazing sun, never making it to the intended area. I apologize to the girls and to my amazement they say, "No problem, Mom. It's kind of fun. It's an adventure!" That's when I know they really embrace our motto and we're all truly on board.

The rest of the book is all about …. What we did.

Touring China

Hong Kong

Our Asian adventure starts in Hong Kong, which I immediately love. To me, Hong Kong is the city money made—you can almost feel the money hanging in the air. Soon, we will see the direct contrast between Hong Kong and mainland China, which to me demonstrates what works, capitalism or communism. Hong Kong is hustle and bustle and everything nice. China is pushing and shoving and struggling to evolve. We see the same lesson in Seoul. Sixty years of U.S. involvement and Seoul's a beautiful, thriving place you want to visit and revisit.

So, go to Hong Kong knowing that it's expensive but worth it. Hong Kong Island, for the most part, is densely populated with clean, sleek, modern high rises shoulder to shoulder especially in the Central area where our hotel is. It feels almost claustrophobic to me, but it's so nice—think luxurious—and there's enough green to make the closeness tolerable.

The harbor is frenetic. I've never seen anything like it except for maybe an ant colony. The city seems so modern and alive to me, but there's an underlying feeling of the past.

Since Britain controlled Hong Kong for more than a hundred and fifty years until 1997, most everyone speaks English and we find the people to be exceptionally nice. To ride the bus, I ask a local woman how much it costs, and she tells me I'll need exact change, which I don't have. She asks several people, exchanges my bills for the right amount, and gets all four of us on the correct bus. Could you ask for more?

When we initially arrive, we withdraw Hong Kong dollars from the ATM at the airport and board a double decker bus—A11—and then transfer to a taxi to get to our hotel. We stay at The Garden View YWCA on MacDonnell Road on Hong Kong Island.

Apparently, the Y's are famous with travelers here. It's a regular, nice hotel with a pool and a reasonable price tag. Plus, it has a super location. Just down the hill is the tram for Victoria Peak, across the street is an outdoor zoo and park (we see twin baby orangutans), and it's a reasonable walk to the Central Midlands Escalators (a series of about twenty escalators conveying people up and down the steep hillside between Queen's Road and Conduit Road). There's also Fusion grocery around the corner with chocolate croissants, apple pastries, sausage buns, yogurt, cheese, and orange juice, to name a few of our favorites.

At the Y, we learn one of our first Asian realities—hotels here offer either two twin beds or a king. There are no double beds unless you stay at expensive Western chains. There also won't be any adjoining rooms. So, we're all in one room. This is the only downside to the Y—one room, four people, two twin beds and not a lot of floor space. This will be our way of life for the next year except—the girls keep growing, which makes the beds seem smaller.

The hotel bathroom is even nicer than most in the U.S. Bathrooms will become a major focal point for us. ... Keep reading.

After leaving our bags at the hotel, we go to Peak Tram and ride to the top of Victoria Peak. On first sight, I'm a mite disappointed because all I see is a partially inhabited observation building with some shopping and some other shops scattered around the grounds. The view is spectacular, but really, I rode at a forty-five-degree angle on a crowded funicular for this?

Then, Jim spots a map of a trail around the Peak—Lugard Road. If you do nothing else in Hong Kong, do this. It's a beautiful flat hike around the Peak with spectacular views, especially of the harbor. Signs describe the flora and fauna, and there are a few surprises like a playground and a ... I'm not going to ruin the surprise.

The hike takes us about an hour and a half because we have to contend with an A one grump—Ella. We attribute the attitude to jet lag and tour on. When her temperature reaches a hundred and three degrees the next day, we realize it's not just jet lag. Yet again, Parent of the Year eludes me.

That night we eat at Pure Veggie House, which like most vegetarian restaurants, is a little different but good. Here we discover another Asian truism. This time, it's about ordering food. I don't know about you but when I was a little girl, my parents told me to eat everything on my plate because the people in China were starving. Well, I hate to admit it, but that was a long time ago and fortunately, things in China have changed. Today, the Chinese show off their wealth by putting an abundance of food on the table.

I think we're pretty typical Americans in that we like to order what we can eat and not waste food or our money. And, trust me, on a budget, you're not going to find a mini fridge in your hotel room to store leftovers. Our advice: Don't listen to the wait staff. Order one fewer dish than they suggest, and then order more if it's not enough.

Another don't-miss tourist attraction in Hong Kong is the Star Ferry between Hong Kong Island and Kowloon. The ferry costs practically nothing and is iconic. You can take the Central-Midlevels Escalator to the pier to board the ferry. The escalators are free and are a great way to get around and see a cool part of the city. In the afternoon, while in Kowloon, have tea at the Intercontinental or another big-name hotel on the harbor to soak in the view of Hong Kong Island. It's a big splurge, but worth it. At night, again from Kowloon, watch the neon light show on the Hong Kong Island skyscrapers. It's something I've never seen anywhere else.

One thing you need to know is that it's practically impossible to cross the street in Hong Kong—too many lanes; too many cars. So, when you start seeing pedestrian crosswalks and inside pathways, get on them. They're there for a reason.

One day we take a double-decker bus to Stanley, on the southern tip of Hong Kong Island. The bus ride itself is an amazing tour of beautiful scenery. Stanley's a beach area where you can swim and hang out. We just walk around and try to get a feel for the place.

There's a famous market here called, predictably enough, Stanley Market. The merchandise we see isn't spectacular, and the prices are high. So, I'm not sure if we found the actual market. However, the scenery and change of pace make the trip worthwhile. We also see the first of many photo shoots. I'm not sure whether it's for a magazine or just a private bridal photo session, but it's definitely entertaining.

Another travel tip: Get your laundry done in Hong Kong. It's convenient, and you pay by the pound. The notion of cheap Chinese laundries has been around a long time, but let me tell you, when you see what the hotels charge, you know that day is long gone. In mainland China, we have a hard time finding laundries, and they charge by the piece. When they see a foreign face, the price goes up even more. So, if you go to China via Hong Kong, get everything cleaned while you can.

Shenzhen

Our next stop is Shenzhen—China's wealthiest city. From Hong Kong, we take the subway and cross the Lo Wu Bridge into mainland China which takes less than an hour. The transition from Hong Kong to mainland China is a big shock. It's so close yet so far. I feel we've left the modern world behind us. And, in many ways, we have….

To be fair, we stay only a night and two days in Shenzhen. I'm also not sure our hotel is in the part of the city to get the best impression. Admittedly, it takes a while to get the lay of the land no matter where you are. But, Shenzhen is no Hong Kong.

Our tour book, *Lonely Planet,* says Shenzhen was made a "Special Economic Zone" in 1980 and is mainly a business center, not a tourist Mecca. I second that. It's frustrating that no one speaks English at our hotel, our Chinese is limited, we're hungry and tired, and it's raining yet hot. No more pampered tourism in Hong Kong, where we could choose to eat any cuisine that came to mind and get by with English. By gosh, we're in a foreign country.

We stay at the GDH Inn for $40 a night. It's okay. We eat breakfast at the restaurant across the street from the hotel. Today, breakfast is noodles and whatever else looks somewhat familiar—egg and tomato soup, green onion crepe, noodle egg roll and bean paste doughnuts.

Ella at breakfast—she's happy. This reminds me that she's Chinese. Her satisfaction with noodles for breakfast must be part of her DNA. I, of course, am longing for my Frosted Mini-Wheats.

Based on advice from *Lonely Planet*, we choose to eat dinner at the Muslim Hotel Restaurant. For the wealthiest city in China, the *Lonely Planet* lists only three restaurants, and they should have left this one off. The service is lousy, the food okay, the tablecloth stained, and bottom line, the restaurant has a weird vibe. The bathrooms give you a sampling. The toilets are holes in the floor, and there's no stall door closure and only half-height partitions between the stalls. It's weird. The girls go in but refuse to use it. They say it's worse than a Porta Jon at a construction site that's never been serviced.

The high point of the evening is the cab ride back to the hotel, where we watch the neon light displays on the buildings. The huge neon shows in some of the Chinese cities are just phenomenal. Shenzhen's is truly a bright spot in a dismal picture.

Jim reads that Shenzhen is a good place to buy electronics and we need a router. So, we spend a good portion of the next morning walking and taking the subway and walking and walking to find the electronics market. Mind you, I'm not tech savvy. So, this is already an uphill battle.

When we finally find the market, it's stall after stall of parts and pieces of parts, which you bargain for. The market goes on and on and on in all directions, and there are multiple floors and buildings that all flow together. Trying to keep track of my family is overload enough, much less trying to figure out what to do with all these parts. We're all just taking it in, but Jim is moving at a fairly good pace.

Take a step back and think about losing your husband and/or a child or two in a labyrinth where you're not sure how to find the entrance or the exit. Imagine you're not sure how to say the name of your hotel and don't know how to get back there. You know, I'm talking about <u>me</u> getting lost. Can you imagine being almost fifty and getting lost—not being able to ask for help or knowing your address? I'm not three, but it sure feels like it. It's a frightening prospect, and I make a concerted effort to hang close to at least one member of my family.

Nobody gets lost, but after this, one of our travel rituals is taking a business card or something from the hotel with its name and address on it wherever we go. This is one of my mandates—everyone must have this information on his or her person. All tourists should do this. When traveling, it seems one person tends to take the lead and everyone else is along for the ride. I'm learning, in a foreign country, especially where words are unrecognizable, everyone really needs to pay attention. Remember, Rose, Ella, and Jim all speak Mandarin well enough to get by… but not me.

Guangzhou

We take a really nice train from Shenzhen to Guangzhou, which takes about an hour and a half. No reservations needed since the trains run every half hour. When we get to the Guangzhou train station, we encounter what will become a very common transportation dilemma: Should we try to figure out the public transportation system or take a "black cab" to our destination? A "black cab" is a guy with a car who says he'll take you to your destination for an inflated price. We see signs warning against this. Nonetheless, we go with the black cab. This results in the kids and me getting out of the car once we reach our destination and Jim paying an amount he thinks is fair but that the cabby has a fit over.

This is the amenity tray at our next hotel near the airport in Guangzhou. You know it's not the Ritz when toilet paper is an amenity. Note the nice touch of the stained tea bag wrapper. Tea anyone? Oh, and finding a nonsmoking room—one that doesn't smell like an ashtray—is a challenge.

Judging by the amenity tray, you know we're on the cheap. Jim's thinking is we don't need a fancy hotel for just one night, and he thinks $30 will get us a fairly nice room. We haven't been in China in eight years and we're realizing China isn't the bargain it used to be. You can't pay $30 and get a decent room anymore in a large city. The hotel (Dongzhi Hotel) does have a small restaurant, where we eat dinner. We order what the people near us are eating, and it's tasty—definitely homemade. It isn't the cleanest place we've ever eaten—in fact, it's probably one of the dirtiest. But we'll eat in a lot of these places in the coming months and when you're hungry, you eat.

What adds to the not-so-niceness of the hotel is the filthy street it's on. We decide to take a walk after dinner to get a feel for the neighborhood and get a little exercise. There's trash blowing around and black dust on everything, no clean surface at any height. The streets are lined with local shops and people are sitting outside eating food from street vendors and open-air restaurants. We get ice cream to help cool ourselves from the heat and to reward ourselves for taking everything in stride.

Rose and Ella have been very good sports about the hotel, the meal and the heat. They say little and just roll with the punches as they usually do, but ice cream has this magic and always elevates all of our moods.

We get our first Magnum bars here. This develops into a family favorite. They come in chocolate, vanilla and a coffee flavor I like, but they're expensive (over $2 each) and not always available.

Over the course of the year, we discover Chinese frozen bars come in some pretty interesting flavors, including pea and corn, which Chinese kids actually like. I'm amazed to see firsthand kids happily eating them. Rose and Ella think these flavors sound disgusting and never sample them. Ella develops a fondness for a banana bar. She peels the gelatin outer layer like a banana to get to the vanilla ice cream center. Rose likes a milk yogurt bar.

Sanya

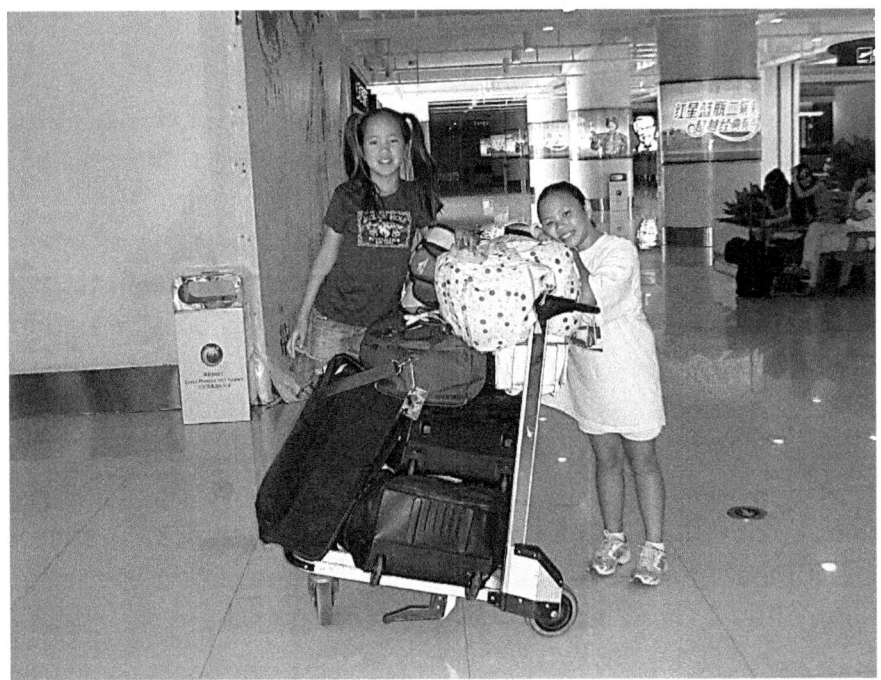

Rose and Ella with all our gear in the Sanya airport

The next morning we take the airport shuttle from the hotel. The shuttle costs $30—no bargain there. Our 9 a.m. flight is non-eventful except for the Chinese children who act as if they're at a park instead of on a plane. They climb over the seats, run up and down the aisle, and are just wild. The parents do nothing. I watch in amazement.

Sanya is on the island of Hainan, just south of mainland China. It is known as "the Hawaii of China." Maybe, if we had stayed at one of the big resort hotels like the MGM Grand where we spend an afternoon, we might have gleaned a likeness. Since we're staying a week, Jim rents an apartment in a very nice complex that is close to ... nothing. Plus, it's surrounded by rubble.

As I heard in a movie once, "China is going to be really nice when they finish construction." That's how Sanya strikes me. Someday all the pieces will come together and it will be really nice.

I digress for a moment to talk about expectations. Yes, our trip is an adventure, good and bad, but when I have certain expectations—like the Hawaii of China—and they're not met, I'm disappointed. On our honeymoon, we went to the "Venice of Portugal" (not), so I should have known better. But this is supposed to be our vacation spot. The place we kick back, relax and soak up the sun. It isn't. And sometimes I get cranky. So, when traveling, check your expectations. Having jet lag doesn't help anything either. On top of being disappointed, I'm tired and this causes extreme crankiness. Thankfully, I'm in the minority. Jim and the girls aren't complaining except when it comes to the squat toilet. Read on ...

There are three things to note about our apartment (Luuhoo Apartments in Sanya City) and the complex. The first is that our apartment has one bathroom, which has a squat toilet. Great—Ella waits two days to use it.

For most traveling Westerners, squat toilets are part of the cultural experience when we're out and about and there's no choice. But where we stay, give us our throne. At every accommodation we stay at from then on, the first thing we do is check the toilet. We breathe a sigh of relief when it's one of our own.

The famous Chinese squat toilet

The second amusing aspect of our accommodation is our balcony. It's growing weeds—lots of weeds. We're on the ninth floor. Old mops and even an old tire are on the balcony beside ours. This is a fairly new condo complex, but it's quickly heading in the stereotypical trailer park direction.

The third interesting finding is a really nice swimming pool, which is the focal point of the complex. Every apartment overlooks it. It's beautiful, immaculate and extremely tempting in the high humidity and high temps of mid-June. However, we never see anyone swim in it. We find out there's a $10-per-person charge that no one can afford. What a waste.

Another thing we come to realize is the beds in China are different. No mattress and box spring on a frame here. The beds appear to be somewhat like a box spring with a board and a wooden platform underneath. No jumping on these beds. We find them a mite hard no matter which way we toss and turn.

There's pretty much nothing within walking distance of the apartment. No shops and only a few sketchy restaurants. It's pretty much building sites and high-rises. Catching a cab is a major feat. And there are no traffic lights, stop signs, or pedestrian crossings for blocks. When there is a pedestrian crossing, we wait for an opening, hold the girls' hands tightly and shout "run."

Our rule of thumb for our entire China experience is to cross the street when the Chinese cross. In China, you're watching out not only for cars but for anything with a wheel. Sanya has an overabundance of motor bikes. Whole families ride on them, including babies and toddlers. Helmets are nonexistent in China along with car seats, booster seats, and seat belts.

During our travels, we see a car seat in a mall on display. It's on a turning pedestal with a spot light on it as if it has fallen from the heavens and no one is quite sure what it is or what to do with it but it's worthy of awe. It's surreal.

Sanya is made up of three distinct beach areas: Sanya Bay in the city, Dadonghai Bay with its boardwalk a little to the east, and Yalong Bay a little more to the east with supposedly the best beach. We try Dadonghai Bay first, gaining access to the boardwalk through Resort in Time Hotel. The boardwalk is right along the beach. It's very nice and busy. It's lined with restaurants with a view of the South China Sea, tropical trees, and men (a lot of Russians) wearing "panties," as Rose and Ella like to call their Speedoesk swimwear.

Rose, Ella, and Jim go for a dip after lunch. The sea is rough but fun. Jim sees something floating that looks like a hand, which freaks him out. A year later, he's still talking about it.

The next day we attempt to find Rainbow Bar and Grill, which is recommended in *Lonely Planet* and promises good American fare. After many modes of transportation—walking, a bus ride, walking, a taxi ride, walking—ice creams and beverages, three hours later we arrive to find the restaurant opens at 4:00 p.m. Only three more hours.

Rainbow Bar and Grill is located on the river with really interesting boats docked along the edges. We find a Chinese resort next to it with several restaurants. So, we lounge in the hammocks and peruse the docks as we wait.

Finally, we give in to hunger and eat at one of the resort's restaurants as we'll do several more times during our stay. Jim really likes a couple of the dishes. Admittedly, it tastes really good to me the first day when we are really hungry but there are so many flies—think horse barn—and it's so hot inside (like a sauna) that it gets to be a joke that Jim wants to eat here. The restrooms have squat toilets just to add to the ambiance.

The English-speaking manager of the hotel intercepts us after we use the lobby restrooms (Western toilets) on one of our visits and asks for our room number. We explain that we really like the (fly-infested) restaurant and have eaten there several times. The manager is a haughty jerk, and I wander off, leaving Jim to make nice and exchange business cards with him.

Let me explain that Chinese "resorts" are not what any Westerner would consider a resort. Most are outdated regardless of when they were built. The lobbies are huge, impersonal, primitive-feeling expanses. The guest rooms are usually large but only offer basic furnishings and minimal decor. There's no golf, tennis, or other activities Western resorts offer.

"Resort" to me connotes luxury, and there is none by Western standards. Now, mind you, there are Western-owned resort chains in China like the MGM Grand, which are truly grand. But even there, quality service is lacking. Service is an area the Chinese have not yet mastered, but that's a story for another day.

All this to say, the manager of the hotel really got under my skin and should have paid us for gracing his crummy property. Yes, I can be ugly when provoked.

Moving on …. Finding a supermarket proves equally frustrating. Jim and the girls use all the Chinese vocabulary they know to describe a place to buy food. We are taken to a fruit market, a pharmacy, and a corner store before a taxi driver finally gets us to a good-sized store to buy some provisions for the rest of the week. In addition to the food items, we buy laundry detergent. Since our apartment has a washing machine, I do our first load of laundry in China and hang it out to dry on the balcony just like all the rest of China.

Some things we take for granted in America, the Chinese don't have. This includes clothes dryers and ovens. Refrigerators are usually smaller—and don't even think about a dishwasher or disposal.

Jim muses that someday the Chinese will stop hanging their laundry in front of their view. I agree. Although I like hanging out wash, I just don't like covering up the only place you can see out and let natural light in.

When we rented a house in Mexico, one of my greatest joys was hanging out the wash on the roof balcony. There was a great view of the park next door, I could hear the music from the dance studio nearby, and there's just something organic about hanging out wash. As I clipped the pins to the clothes, I fantasized I was an actress in an Italian movie. It was lovely. However, our Mexican house was four stories with an open-air house plan that included several large balconies, French doors, and windows galore. This provided lots of places to let the sunshine in and see out. This is not the case in China.

The Foreigners Are in 709

As we are going to bed that night around 9:30, there is a knock at the door. Jim answers it, and I can hear him speaking Chinese with two other men. He asks me for the passports—I'm the designated passport holder. I recommend everybody have one of these—and he quickly leaves. I go to bed and wake several times wondering if we'll ever see Jim again and if we're now in the midst of some Asian spy thriller. Yes, I'm worried and my imagination goes a little wild, but I'm also too tired to get out of bed and do anything about it.

Of course, Jim returns safe and sound with a reasonable story about four hours later. He was taken to the apartment office to register our passports since we are foreigners. This is common practice when checking into a hotel in another country, but in this instance, the circumstances are a little unusual.

Jim is put in a car and driven to another part of town where a central renting office is located. Then, Jim's captors have copier and computer problems, which take hours to resolve. And why Jim is taken off at night the day after we arrive instead of when we pick up the key is a little odd. Most of the mystery is explained away by the fact that these apartments are seldom, if ever, rented to foreigners. This also may explain the squat toilets.

The next day we take buses—yes, plural—to the Sanya Bay beach area. We miss the stop for the nicer resort and end up eating lunch at an OK Chinese resort. Remember, we are using the term resort loosely.

A Chinese tour group is also eating here. Let's just say it's obvious that others have eaten at our table, and the plates they bring us are wet and chipped. I consider this a bit gross, but we are beginning to accept this as our new normal. We have a dish with chicken where the bone is sliced through along with the meat. We'll see this a lot too, but I never get used to it. Along with this, we have a chewy beef dish with rice we request to have served with the beef. We have learned that rice traditionally arrives well after the meat course. The way we eat Chinese food in America is not how the Chinese eat it in China.

As we chew, we watch the tables the tour group was seated at being cleared. I find this both interesting and disgusting. I grew up with a mother who didn't allow us to stack plates as they were being removed from the table much less scraped. I remember this as I watch the plates and serving dishes being scraped of all contents into a bucket at each table. This should not happen at a resort. We eat our meal, and I avert my eyes to the pool area. The meal costs $28 for the four of us.

After lunch, we go for a swim and lounge by the resort's pool for a bit. There are very few people, mainly Russians, and we easily get chairs. Things get lively when two local teenage boys jump in and security tries to get them out. It's a little Keystone Copish because the boys are in the water out of grasp and security isn't dressed for a swim and perhaps doesn't know how to swim—many Chinese don't know how to swim, for lack of opportunity. Finally, the boys get out with security yelling, waving their hands and chasing them. We feel a little guilty since we're basically doing the same thing as the boys.

We nonchalantly slink off and find the beach. And, I must say from this vantage point, I can understand the Hawaii reference. The beach is beautiful with a view of the Sanya skyline. Jim and the girls go for a swim. I find the Beach Bar, where we eat a snack and drink several wonderful Mai Tais. There are very few people on the beach, this being the low season. However, massages and trinkets are still available from strolling beach vendors.

That night we eat dinner at Rainbow Bar and Grill. We order and eat a club sandwich, chicken tenders, Hawaiian pizza, onion rings, French fries, and a banana split sundae. It's expensive but tastes just like home. We're happy.

The next day we take bus #24 ($2.50 for the four of us) to the Sheraton at Yalong Bay beach. This is considered one of the best resorts in Sanya. The grounds are well manicured with exotic, blooming tropical plants. The restaurant setting is upscale. We have beautifully plated food complete with fresh flowers and handblown sugar decorations as garnishes, but the food itself is just OK, the portions are small, and all-in-all not worth the $90 bill.

We are turned away from their pool by the lifeguard but meander down the beautiful grounds to the beach where Jim and the girls swim and play in the surf. I watch a woman maneuvering a Segway in the sand. This I have never seen before.

We then enter the MGM Grand pool area, which is quite spectacular with infinity pools, waterfalls and statuary.

We order snacks and fruity tropical drinks and totally enjoy ourselves until the sky opens and pelts us with rain as we run for cover.

I sigh and think how nice it would be to forget about our two-bedroom, $47-a-night apartment in Sanya City and get a room at the MGM Grand. Jim just smiles and counts the savings.

The next day the winds are high, and red flags are flying on the beach to warn of rip tides. It pours rain while we watch Chinese TV to pass the time and pack our bags. We are ready to leave. Next stop is back to Guangzhou, where we meet our guide for Ella's orphanage tour.

We get to the airport the next morning only to find all flights have been canceled due to the "monsoon." We meet another American couple who have been living in China for the past three years. The husband is with IBM and travels a lot. So, I trust him when he explains that flight cancellations are common and usually due to

Chinese military maneuvers but are always attributed to the weather.

We are bused away for lunch and checked into a hotel for the night with the rest of our stranded traveling companions. The next day the people in charge inform us that we will be stranded for yet another day.

This is very upsetting. Ella's orphanage tour is scheduled for the next day and if we miss it, we can't reschedule for any time in the near future. It takes special permission from the government to visit an orphanage, and everything has been arranged and paid for.

Jim forges ahead and somehow manages to get us checked out, to the airport and on a flight to Guangzhou later that day. I have no explanation for this. When we land, the most welcome sight I have seen in a long time is a sign with "Young" on it. Our orphanage tour guide, Alvin, is waiting for us. We gather our luggage, count it, and move on.

Guangzhou and Ella's Orphanage

We spend the night at the Guangzhou Victory Hotel on Shamian Island, which is part of Guangzhou. This is very familiar territory since we stayed at the White Swan Hotel on Shamian Island during our daughters' adoptions. The White Swan is a five-star-rated hotel with a multi-story waterfall in the lobby, chic shops and multiple restaurants overlooking the Pearl River. During this visit, it's closed for renovation. Unfortunately, the Victory is no White Swan, but it's OK.

The next day our guide and our driver take us to Qingxin, where Ella's orphanage is located. Qingxin is surrounded by mountains and is about an hour and a half car ride northeast of Guangzhou. We spend the night at the Grace Gardens Hotel, which has elaborate grounds and OK rooms. I think we could have done this visit as a one-day trip, but ... we didn't.

The trip is arranged through Always and Forever Adoption Homeland Tours. The cost for the guide, driver, accommodations, meals, and sightseeing is $1,260 for approximately three days. In addition, there is a facilitating fee of $100, and we paid a fee of 900 yuan ($150) for filing the orphanage visit petition with Guangdong Civil Affairs. Tips for the driver and guide are also expected.

The orphanage where Ella lived has been relocated to the outskirts of town. So, first thing in the morning, we go to the new location, where we are warmly greeted by one of the women who originally brought us Ella on her adoption day. Several of the women speak very good English, the facility is very nice, and the few children who are there look very well cared for. Almost all of them have visible handicaps.

To our surprise, the woman who found Ella as a baby in the outdoor market and brought her to the police station is here—Mrs. Xiao. Mrs. Xiao is overjoyed to see Ella. As she is hugging her and crying, Ella is mouthing, "She's choking me. Can we go now?" I want to throttle my child and hope that someday, when she is not nine, she will remember and appreciate this day.

The orphanage prepares a very traditional, abundant, Chinese lunch complete with a whole fish, a special soup from the region, and multiple courses. The staff, Mrs. Xiao, we, and our

entourage eat at a huge, round, wooden table with the food passed on a lazy Susan. Everything is so pleasant. In my eyes, this is a perfect visit.

Ella is pictured with the staff of the orphanage and Mrs. Xiao, who is second from the left

Next, we visit Ella's finding site, which is no longer an outdoor market but the site of a department store. Again, Ella is bored and wants to move on. I look around at the surrounding apartment buildings and wonder if someone knows or saw something the day Ella was left. Tears fill my eyes and I hope her mother knows Ella is a beautiful, smart, happy child, who is very loved ... even when I want to throttle her.

We return to Guangzhou and the Victory Hotel for two more nights. We do some sightseeing with live scorpions and dried seahorses being the highlights. This is Jim's and my third visit to Guangzhou, and I still don't feel like I have a handle on it. For whatever reason, I also don't have a desire to know more.

So, back to the hotel, where the pool is a sight to behold. It's on the top floor of the hotel and is built right next to the edge of the building with only an open metal railing around it. I feel compelled to get a picture of the girls swimming in the pool. But with safety a chief concern, they aren't allowed near the railing.

It's just too inconceivable that anyone would build a pool like this. I like this aspect of China to some degree. Everything doesn't come with a warning and everyone isn't suing everyone else over coffee being too hot or some other ridiculous thing you should know not to do. So, they have some things we would never have in the U.S., and it makes me smile.

We take the overnight train from Guangzhou to Shanghai. Guangzhou's train station is big but not the nicest. The bathrooms are smelly with squat toilets that haven't been cleaned in a while. The waiting area is packed with mainly migrant workers who are very nice and especially curious about us and the girls. We chat with them as best we can.

Of course, someone in our group is always hungry. To get to the snack store in our waiting area, we high-step over the huge burlap sacks stuffed with the migrants' belongings.

The store is stocked mainly with things we don't normally eat. At most train stations, we can usually find peanuts, peanut M&Ms, crackers, and sometimes some chips we like. The Chinese have very different taste in chips—many are seafood flavored. If nothing else, there are usually ramen noodle bowls we can buy. Each of the train stations has a hot water faucet in the lounge area used to rehydrate the noodles.

Shanghai

We survive the nineteen-hour train ride. It isn't bad. We are in a sleeper with four bunks, so we don't share the compartment with anyone else. The girls love it and insist on the top bunks— "Oh, no, not the top bunks. Your dad and I really want them." Right. Our sheets are clean, and there is a Western toilet in our car.

However, the bathroom reeks. (The Chinese put toilet paper in the trash; not the toilet. The sewage systems weren't built to handle paper.) Also, the comforter and carpet in our compartment have stains—TMI, right? Ella and I sleep with shower caps on our heads (just in case), and Jim and I sleep in our sleep sacks. I also take a sleeping pill, which makes everything OK.

When traveling like the locals, you're likely to meet a few. A young man, Sun, who wants to practice his English, attaches himself to us almost immediately. One minute he's in the hallway charging his phone, and the next minute he's in our sleeper making an origami rose for the girls and we're just talking about China, the U.S., food, etc., for hours. It's hard to know how to say enough, but he gets the hint eventually, says goodnight, and leaves. Sun (our new best friend) meets us the next day to show us how to navigate the Shanghai subway.

So, on day one in Shanghai, we walk the Bund (the famous road along the Huangpu River, which runs through Shanghai), eat at one of the *Lonely Planet*-recommended restaurants (South Memory), which is dirty by Western standards and expensive. It's located in the trendiest mall around on East Nanjing Road, which is a huge pedestrian street. We also take the girls to a small amusement park and then collapse in our room at the Oriental Bund Hotel. The Oriental Bund is one of our better accommodation choices—with Western toilets (the girls cheer and clap as we walk into the room and spot the toilet), wall-mounted, big-screen TV, it's clean, and has a great location ($80). We also have internet service. Plus, our Vonage phone is working which means we can call home if we want. Hope and the girls are happy equals Jim is happy. We'll be here for five nights.

Here we are on the pedestrian walkway along the Bund. The Huangpu River and the iconic images of the area known as Pudong are in the background.

The Foreigners Are in 709

This is the first time I feel like there are REALLY a LOT of people in China. Feeling the closeness of people and how quickly my loved ones can disappear into the masses is a little overwhelming—East Nanjing Road—but check out the great architecture.

We ride in these very prevalent, somewhat dangerous, but REALLY fun three-wheeled vehicles to get back to the hotel. Ella and I race Jim and Rose and win. If you're interested in riding in these carts, Shanghai is the place to do it because these contraptions aren't in abundance in other cities, at least ones we visit.

It's cloudy with some rain most of the time we're in Shanghai, but we buy cheap umbrellas and persevere. My favorite tourist site is the Yuyuan Garden. It's what you picture in your mind when you think of Chinese gardens and architecture. It's a photographer's dream if you can snap the shot between people.

This dragon is part of the wall in the garden

We really like the French Concession area of Shanghai and find The Commune Restaurant, which has unusually good casual Western food. The soups are great, and the fresh fruit juices are out-of-this-world good. We eat here twice. The tiny shops in this maze of alleys are filled with things I want to buy. It's a trendy, hip area worth checking out. I keep looking for an area like this in Beijing but never find anything quite as good.

We also explore other attractions such as the 2010 World Expo Site, which is a ghost town now. We walk a lot and find none of the buildings open. Not surprisingly, it's also very difficult to find a taxi. We pay to see the Shanghai Museum, but there's an overabundance of things to see and read. We find it very two-dimensional without interactive exhibits and our girls aren't engaged—at all. We give in to the whining and leave.

During the next two days, our friend Jane joins us, and she's like a breath of fresh air. Jane's from China but she's very Americanized. She's a Wake Forest student we hosted one summer while she interned in Charlotte and we now think of her as part of our family. She's one of those rare people everyone likes no matter their age.

With Jane and her high school friend, Sun (no relation to our friend on the train), we visit the Shanghai Ocean Aquarium on the Pudong side of the river. It's a nice aquarium, but we've been to the Atlanta aquarium and just recently to the one in Charleston, S.C. So, by this time, unless we get to swim with the dolphins, we're pretty much over it. Also, the Shanghai aquarium is expensive—about $27/person.

Afterward, we duck out of the rain into a mega mall looking for a traditional Chinese jade bangle bracelet for

Jim to give me for my fiftieth birthday. This proves to be overwhelming. How do we know if it's real jade? How much should we pay? What shade of green should I get? Jane calls her mother for advice. Her mother says it's hard to know. and she recommends buying one from a reputable store. So, we bag the shopping and give in to hunger.

We learn that these mega malls have wonderful food courts in the basements. Jane introduces us to Chinese hot pot. She instructs us on how to order and how to eat it. It's pretty much a water-based fondue, but we never would have been able to order without Jane's help. Each of us has our own individual built-in hot pot and from the ingredients Jane orders, we cook and eat what we like. We find hot pot is a great comfort food, especially on this rainy day.

Sun is a very good sport and hangs with us the whole day. He's also a student at an American university and speaks fluent English. Unfortunately, Ella is again running a fever but bucks up because she doesn't want to miss a day with Jane.

After lunch, I find a jade bead necklace that I can wrap multiple times around my wrist and wear as a bracelet. I like this much better than the solid bangle style, which I discover makes me feel claustrophobic. Not being able to easily take something off, regardless of what it is, gives me anxiety and these bangles are tight.

In China, the jade bangle is a symbol of longevity and the life cycle. It is believed to bestow health, luck and happiness to the wearer. Many are passed down through the generations and many people never take them off. Jane had to have hers cut off. Jim purchases the jade necklace at a jewelry store named Chow Tai Fook. From then on, we joke that we got fooked.

On June 29, we celebrate my birthday (which is actually July 1) because there's a special treat in Shanghai. We check into the Waldorf Astoria on the Bund for twenty-four hours of luxury. I'm so happy that I almost can't stand it. It's incredible. I don't think I would have appreciated this as much in the U.S. or if I hadn't experienced the other end of the hotel spectrum so recently. I am overjoyed. This rates as one of my best birthdays ever, and I'm one of those people who take celebrating one's birth seriously—it should be a really good day. Little do I know that my next birthday will be one of my worst....

The day is great because:

1. I wake up looking at a blue sky. We haven't seen blue sky in a week because of the rain and gray skies. We're beginning to suspect pollution.

2. The Supreme Court upholds the healthcare law (Affordable Care Act)—I'm so tired of the controversy.

3. Our room at the Waldorf is incredible. All of us share in this joy. The round bathroom window goes from clear to opaque, and the drapes close with the push of a button. Then, there's the toilet — it has a built-in bidet. It's high-tech with all the buttons to rinse you, dry you and raise, lower, and heat the seat. It makes Rose laugh. Frankly, it

delights us all—who knew a toilet could do this? We'll see these toilets again in Japan and South Korea, but we'll forever call them Waldorf toilets.

4. Unsolicited goodies—a birthday cake, cookie tray and fresh pears—greet us as we return to our room from the beautiful, huge, indulgent, breakfast buffet.

5. Child-sized Waldorf robes arrive at our door for the girls. When we crash other resort pools, the guests have all been wearing their hotel emblemed robes and quite honestly, we have robe envy. With our robes on, we have finally arrived, and we traipse off to the pool.

6. Jim books a two-hour head-to-toe massage for me in the French Concession area (Shanghai Sooth Wind

Massage). It costs around $10/hour with no tipping allowed. Is this not the best birthday ever?

7. After a nice Italian dinner in the French Concession, we order a drink at The Long Bar, which is the Waldorf's historic lounge. Both hotel managers come by and ask the girls if it's a special occasion. Champagne and other bubbly drinks appear, along with snacks, as the management toasts my birthday. This place rocks.

Hangzhou and High-Speed Trains

We take Jane up on her invitation to visit her hometown of Hangzhou. Hangzhou has the reputation of being the coolest city in China and having some of the best cuisine. We know Jane as a sophisticated, international twenty-one-year-old. So, it will be interesting to meet her parents and see her on her own turf. We end up staying three days.

We take the high-speed train, which gets us to Hangzhou in about an hour. These trains are the best and are becoming available in more Chinese cities. They are new, clean, punctual, and save so much time. They're also still very affordable. These trains even have the equivalent of flight attendants selling snacks and helping with seats and luggage.

Jane books our room at a hotel (Hangzhou Sunny Huansha Hotel on Huansha Road) within walking distance to her parents' apartment, which is within walking distance to West Lake and a nice mall. Jane is the perfect hostess; she arrives each morning to lay out our day and spends the day showing us the sights. Our hotel room is her parents' treat.

Jane first takes us to West Lake, which is a huge park around a lake—of course. Hangzhou dates back to 221 BC. So, many things have come and gone, including elements of West Lake. West Lake is highly reconstructed, but it holds true to classic details of ancient, ornate China. We see the iconic golden water buffalo, willow and plum trees, lotus flowers, pagodas, half-moon and zigzag bridges, and old-style Chinese boats.

Jane, Rose, Ella and me at West Lake. Note the beautiful bridge and golden water buffalo sculpture in the background

It's a very hot July day, and we stroll with our umbrellas open for shade just like the rest of the Chinese masses who have come to enjoy the outdoors. We get drinks and ice cream and hop on the tram ($6.50/person) that circles the lake. We come back at night for the one-and-a-half-hour boat cruise.

On the cruise, Jim and I are hit with the realization that we have no idea what's going on around us. We drift into our own little worlds. When we are nudged back to consciousness, I notice we're both looking to the right and everyone else (and I mean toddlers, old people and everyone in between; even our children) is looking intently at something to the left. So much for a guided tour. In our defense, the guide is speaking Chinese.

The other Hangzhou site we particularly enjoy is the old pedestrian street, Qinghefang. There are interesting crafts and candy-making demonstrations on the street as well as tons of shops with traditional Chinese ware and restaurants with Chinese fare. Jane buys a pastry called Ding Sheng Gao to share and explains that it's believed that if you eat this pastry before an exam you'll do well. We go to the Chinese Medicine Museum also on Qinghefang, which is still operating as a clinic. It looks really interesting, but it's all in Chinese so we mosey on.

As you can see, outside the Medicine Museum, things are not always harmonious among us. According to Ella, "Rose is being annoying." But according to Rose, "Ella, can't take a joke." We're all a bit hot and tired. Time to eat.

Part of our order has arrived—dumplings, soup, and a tofu dish. We usually stick to food we somewhat know—dumplings, chicken dishes, soup and rice—so it's nice to be guided into new territory. Jane orders a famous Hangzhou dish called Dong Po Rou. From here on out, we'll eat this dish wherever we can find it. It's not for the health conscious and sounds horrible—pork with a thick layer of fat on top—but it's really delicious. You eat fat and all.

The second evening we're invited to join Jane's parents and friends at a restaurant for dinner. There's so much food on the table, and more keeps arriving. Drinking is very much part of the evening. "Gambai" is the traditional toast, which means "bottoms up" and it's repeated in quick succession throughout the meal. Jim and I take a shot or two and retire. The liquor being shot is the equivalent of grain alcohol.

Every dish is put on a huge lazy Susan and spun around for everyone to enjoy. Rose is eating some unknown food, and we ask Jane to tell us what it is. At first, she just says, "I'm not telling you." When Rose agrees it's good, Jane tells us it's pig tail. Yes, the tail of a pig. Sometimes you just need to try what's in front of you. The Chinese make incredible sauces, which make so many things delicious.

We learn a lot from this meal that holds true throughout our visit. The Chinese eat many things the average

American can't even imagine, including almost every part of an animal. I believe this originates from when food was scarce, which wasn't that long ago. My friend Jenny's grandmother starved to death during the Cultural Revolution. Plus, each part of the animal is thought to aid some part of the human body and prevent a particular ailment. This is just like us saying, "Eat your carrots; they're good for your eyesight." But I mean EVERYTHING has a specific benefit according to the Chinese.

I believe the Chinese get more nutrients by eating this way. However, I just can't eat a fish eye. Sometimes it's all in the marketing—I don't like liver, but pate is amazing. Maybe I'd like eye pate.

As you know from the American version of Chinese food, most everything is chopped into bite-sized pieces. I believe this is for at least two reasons: 1. You can eat bite-sized pieces easily with chop sticks—no table knives required. 2. The majority of Chinese have been poor for a long time, and chopped food looks like you have more.

Fish tanks

Other things of note about Chinese cuisine include encountering fish tank displays when entering most restaurants. This way you can choose the exact sea creature you want, and ... it's fresh. They even bring it to your table in a plastic bag for you to double-check and show you it's still swimming, crawling, snapping, or whatever. Very fresh. The funny thing is the plastic bag they carry the creature in is a used grocery or shopping bag, not a new, fresh, sanitized bag. On the bright side, it's going to be cooked, so no germ worries ... right?

In this vein, we find one restaurant in Guangzhou that has a variety of live insects in plastic wash tubs you can order. I'm not sure whether they bring them to the table before cooking them. We didn't eat there. Again, bugs are probably very nutritious and delicious, but I'm just not going there.

Most Chinese food is inexpensive, which promotes over-ordering behavior. Apparently, we're not the only ones who notice this trend. While we're in China, a government campaign begins, urging people not to waste food. I see an ad in a newspaper with this message.

Believe it or not, Western food is expensive and incredibly, these people who can master delicate sauces usually can't cook a decent hamburger and fries. We never have the opportunity to sample a steak. But with a hamburger plate costing around $20, I'd hate to think what a filet mignon would cost.

Back to attractions, one of our biggest let-downs as far as sights go occurs when we ask Jane to take us to a "water town." This is no fault of Jane's, just a mixture of weather, people, nothing in English and expectations of discovering a cool, out-of-the- way place. I come to realize that no place in China is going to be "undiscovered"—hello, there are over a billion people here.

Jane books us on a day tour of Wuzhen, which consists of a restored town circa the Qing Dynasty on a network of waterways. Some original residents still live here, but mostly it's set up for tourists.

We arrive by bus after a mandatory stop at a multi-level gem and jewelry store. This is so Chinese. Chinese tours are notorious for making stops at mega stores where "fabulous" deals can be had. Be aware that the tour company or guide is getting a cut of your purchases. This also happens with our orphanage guide. You would think a guide you personally hire would be trying to get you the best deals, but not so. I don't like this.

It doesn't help our Wuzhen tour that it's a sweltering day, but the main pitfall is there are so many tourists in this little town that you can't see anything but the tops of heads, umbrellas and buildings. I'm afraid I might be trampled if I fall out of step—no joke. And then there's my concern about getting lost again. So much for discovering an unexplored, quaint town.

We follow along—par usual, the tour is in Chinese, so I don't get a lot out of it. I do get a few good photos from bridges. It's a charming, small, old town when you can get a glimpse.

As soon as we are given free time, we head for a lunch spot. We're lucky because we're seated under a fan and we beat the crowd. Jane helps us order and we have an interesting, filling meal. Again, the table cloth is stained, and the dishes arrive wet and chipped, which is still a bit uncomfortable for me, but at least we are out of the heat.

To help with my sanitary concerns, Jim and the girls have given me a pair of screw-together chop sticks for my birthday. They are wooden and have their own pouch, which conveniently fits into my purse. I no longer need to ponder the cleanliness of restaurant chop sticks or worry about littering the world with disposable ones.
I never knew I had these hang-ups about cleanliness. As you've undoubtedly noticed, the hygiene theme keeps reappearing. However, my friends will tell you I'm the one who eats at the "C-rated" restaurants in the U.S.

This is one of the dishes we have for lunch. It's cooking outside the restaurant door. Believe it or not, this doesn't bother me. I convince myself that the pot has a patina that enhances the flavor and that the pot's so hot, no bacteria or incidental insects can survive.

After lunch, we look around at some of the tourist shops, which have a lot of cheap junk, and head for the bus lot. We end up spending the last hour and a half at the Kentucky Fried Chicken in air conditioning. Again, eating ice cream. I have never spent as much time in KFCs or subsidiaries and eating soft-serve ice cream as I will in China.

Jane says the government limits visitors to Wuzhen to 10,000 people per day. Word to the wise, when you see rows upon rows of tour buses in the parking lot, there are going to be a lot of people. Someone else—maybe most of China—has discovered the charming spot you want to visit. Also, be aware that even though it's crowded, many tourist sites in China don't cater to foreigners yet. So, don't expect English-speaking tours or even English headsets or brochures. To be fair, we were probably the only non-Asian tourists there that day.

This is the row with our bus. Travel tip—take a picture of your bus. Believe me, it's hard to remember which one's yours after you get off, spend the day in the sun, and notice there are over 200 buses that look just like yours.

On the bus ride back, Jane dodges the shopping trip promising once-in-a-lifetime deals on all things silk. She explains to the guide that our hotel is nearby. We leave the tour in the shop's parking lot and high tail it to the hotel.

Nanjing

Jane's mom takes us to the train station the next morning in the Mercedes Jim tells me retails for over one hundred thousand. After our goodbyes and thank you's, we head for Nanjing.

In Guangzhou, I spoke with some Americans who had just adopted their children in Nanjing. They stayed at the Nanjing Aqua City Holiday Inn and based on this, we stay there, too. It's a nice hotel attached to a mega mall. This makes finding a place to eat and buying necessities easy. Since we spent three unexpected days in Hangzhou, we're in Nanjing for only one night, so we head for the biggest tourist site in town. We pay the entrance fee and walk up and on a remnant of the old city wall. There are some signs in English to explain details of the wall, which is great.

This is a section of the old city wall. The steps were built so the generals could ride their horses up them.

The unexpected main event in Nanjing is getting Rose's hair cut. We call Jane, who tells the stylist how Rose wants her hair. The young man spends over an hour cutting and styling. The final bill—$8, and when we try to tip because he does such a great job, he hands it back to us. Tipping is not expected or normal in China. At this point in China, hair care is very professional and cheap. The salons are beautiful. If you have straight hair, go for it. You'll get one of the best cuts of your life.

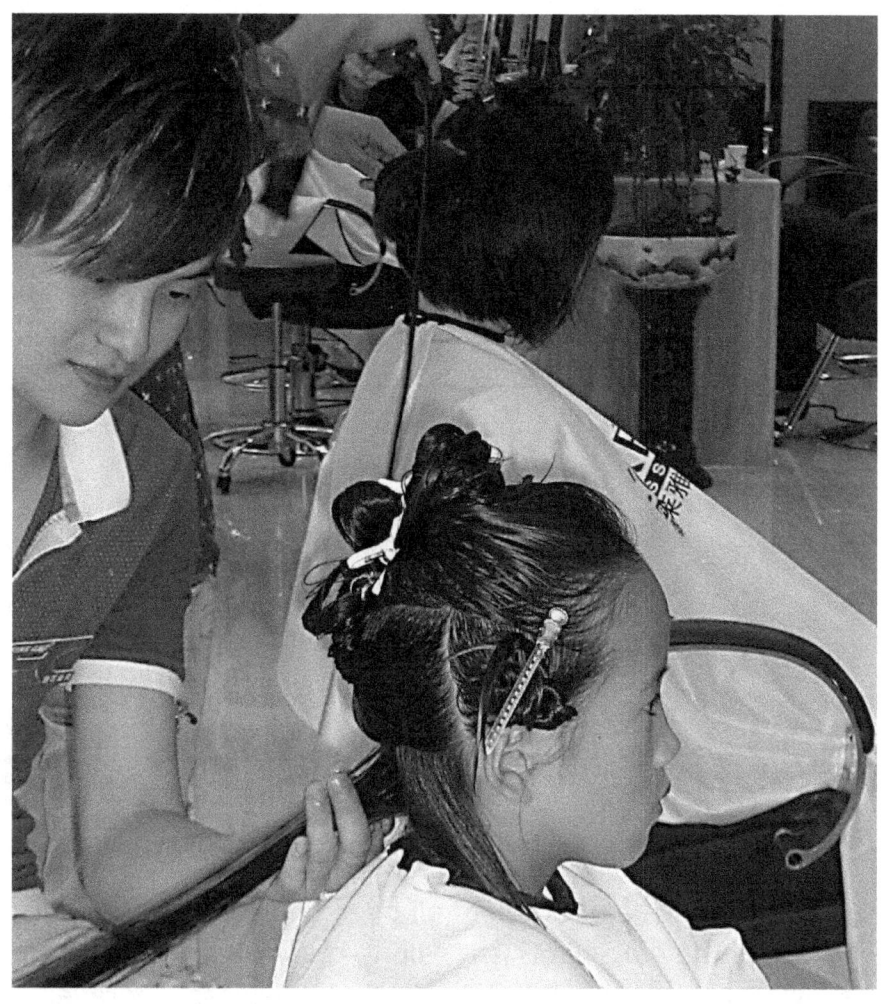

Rose's haircut

One little boy at the mall in split pants

You see babies and toddlers all over China in split pants. Literally, they are pants split along the crotch seam to allow little ones the ability to do their business wherever. Split pants are an alternative to diapers. You do see some diapers, but they're expensive, and think of all the disposable diapers China would need. Traditionally, split pants have been the norm. It takes me until Nanjing to figure out how to get this modest photo of split pants without upsetting anyone.

And, yes, those puddles are pee. On our first trip to China, we were in a nice department store in the children's section, and to our astonishment, a child peed right in the middle of the floor. A janitor quickly but nonchalantly came out and mopped it up. And, no one except Jim and I gaped in amazement.

Hefei and Rose's Orphanage

We take the train from Nanjing to Hefei (in Anhui province), where we will meet up with our guides for Rose's orphanage tour. We find the Holiday Inn where we are meeting the tour guide and driver. Again, this tour is arranged through Always and Forever Adoption Homeland Tours. For two nights in a hotel, the guide, the driver, the van, and most meals, the cost is $825 with an additional $100 facilitating fee and 1,000 yuan ($166) paid to Anhui Civil Affairs for filing the orphanage visit petition.

Finding the hotel takes a while because there are several Holiday Inns in Hefei and it's not the one we thought it was. When we adopted Rose, we ate lunch at the Holiday Inn with the revolving top floor. That's not the one we're booked in this time.

Our hotel room is big, but—as we're now known to say quite often—it's not the Waldorf or even a Holiday Inn as we know them. It just doesn't feel clean and is very basic. Our guide and the driver are staying somewhere less expensive. I honestly feel sorry for them.

The Foreigners Are in 709

We leave around 9 a.m. for Rose's orphanage in Huainan, which is about two hours by car. We were not allowed to visit the orphanage when we adopted Rose. However, we have a sense of it. Our adoption agency arranged for us to send a disposable camera to the orphanage before the adoption. From this, we have about ten pictures of Rose outside and inside the orphanage with different care givers.

We turn off the paved road onto a rutted dirt road. As we bump along in the new minivan, I start to notice large dirt mounds to the left. They go on and on, now on both sides, and I notice some tomb stones on top. The guide tells us they are the graves from the Japanese invasion (we know it as World War II). This is a reminder of the huge number of lives specific to this region that were brutally lost. Somehow, Rose's ancestors survived. This pretty much sets the tone for the rest of the visit—depressing and enlightening.

This is not Ella's orphanage. No one who works here speaks English, and there are lots of children—over three hundred. The children are starving for attention, and the facility is—basic. The grounds are littered with trash.

Of the three hundred children, about half are in foster homes. The children we see are all ages, up to fourteen. Many look totally healthy, but we're told most have had some sort of health problem and haven't been available for adoption.

I have a hard time believing this excuse. We're told several children are in the process of being adopted, but I find it profoundly sad that many of these children could have been adopted already. Any of their health problems could have been resolved more quickly with state-of-the-art medical attention elsewhere.

Whatever the reason, keeping them here is not in the best interest of the children. I break down and sob at one point. I can't understand why so many children are here when I know so many people who want to adopt. I don't understand why adoption from China is taking years when there are children who need a family and families who want these children. It disgusts me that some bureaucracy is ruining all these lives.

Rose at the entrance to the orphanage

On a somewhat lighter note, I want to hold the children, but I hesitate because they have scabs all over them. I believe this is mainly from mosquito bites. I try to balance my selfish need not to catch something (and need medical treatment in a land where Western medicine is not the norm or easily accessible), worrying about transmitting something to my children, and trying to give some of my time and attention to children who are literally begging to be noticed and held. I finally give in to one little special-needs guy about four years old who is holding on to my leg and looking up at me. I figure if he has something contagious, I probably already have whatever it is and should be a better person.

Gradually, I walk over to another group of children who want to speak English. If I could just take a child without years of paperwork, I would have taken the little seven-year-old boy that locked eyes with me and smiled. In our twenty-minute encounter, he steals part of my heart. I hope he finds a happy life.

Prior to our visit, we purchased small gifts, candy and school supplies for the children totaling about $100. As we hand them out, the children are very aggressive. Small fights break out among some of them and, truthfully, I'm a little frightened. I feel as if they might take me out over a trinket.

It hits me that they have to grab and fight. They have nothing of their own. Mom and Dad aren't going to make it better by buying them something else later. These crappy little plastic toys and cheap candy really mean something to them. Not in a "keepsake I'm going to treasure this" way but in an "I got ten sweet things to eat today and a plastic figure I can hold onto until someone steals it from me" way. It's hard to imagine a life where you have nothing and no one. They've learned to fend for themselves, and it scares me.

In one of the rooms, there is a twenty-day-old infant. She is underweight with a profusion of black hair. This was Rose ten years ago. I'm allowed to hold her. I'm told she's being adopted by Americans. I hope the best for her. I think Rose has gotten a pretty sweet deal.

While I'm holding the little bundle, my travel group sees lunch—watery gruel. Literally, this is how the guide and my children describe it. Our guide explains to the orphanage staff that we can't stay for lunch. We leave with me praying that those children somehow find a better life and that China will change its adoption policies. I do want to note that a new facility is being built, and this facility will be closed. I feel selfish and relieved to be leaving.

Our next stop is Rose's finding place, which is described in her adoption paperwork as the gate of a hospital. We discover that "a gate" just means the entrance. As we're wandering around the entrance, we encounter a security guard who has worked there for the past twenty years. Our guide asks him to recommend a local restaurant. He leads us to one and then proceeds to eat with us as our guest. We're seated in a private room upstairs. The restaurant is a bit iffy, but the food is plentiful, definitely fresh—and we're hungry.

We ask the guard some questions through our guide. He says it was very common ten to fifteen years ago for babies to be born at the hospital and, in the case of girls, to leave them the next day on the steps. So, we are almost sure we've found Rose's birthplace. There are no records, however. No computers, and paper files are kept for only five years.

As the food is placed on the table, the guide asks me why I'm not eating the chicken soup. I explain that we're not used to having the whole chicken served in the soup. She quickly stands up, cuts off the head and one leg. After splashing around in the soup, she giggles and says, "It must be a handicapped chicken. There's only one leg!" She thinks this is incredibly funny and repeats it several times.

Jim has placed a potato wedge over the chicken's face

What I think is even funnier is Ella's realization as we're leaving the restaurant grounds and she says, "Mommy, there were three chickens here when we went in and only two now." I just say, "Yes, Ella, you're right." The expression on her face as she realizes she just ate the missing chicken is priceless.

I have never seen our children move so fast in my life. After lunch, the girls need to use the restroom. We're guided out through the kitchen backdoor to the community bathroom. I stay near the kitchen door while the guide shows the girls in and Jim goes to the men's side. In a matter of seconds, the girls are like bullets being shot from the bathroom, both running and saying loudly in unison, "We can wait." Jim, of course, doesn't see why they won't use the bathrooms. Let's just say I could smell the restrooms on approach and decided not to venture closer.

Men—do they have a sense of smell or a sense of cleanliness? I just want to add for background that I never in our year in China used a community bathroom; but practically every time we turned around, Jim was in one. Maybe he's part dog.

We take a leisurely drive back to Hefei, stopping at the famous piano shaped building and walking the grounds. The girls find a cleaner restroom, and we move on.

Back in Hefei, I ask to stop at the Novotel, where we stayed when we adopted Rose. The babies were brought to us at the hotel, and the adoptions were completed in the hotel conference room. We reenact our first encounters with Rose.

We search the park across the street for the spot where we took the family photo we included in Rose's birth announcement. The girls discover brightly colored, big, plastic inflatable tubes that float on the lake. We rent one and the girls have a great time. We are delighted to find these in parks in other cities as well.

Rose and Ella are resting in the inflatable. Most of the time the girls look as if they're on a hamster wheel as they try to climb the sides of the tube.

The next day we leave for Beijing by way of Nanjing, where we catch a fast train. I love these trains.

Arriving in Beijing

We arrive in Beijing as tourists. We stay just off Wangfujing Street, which is a touristy central pedestrian street. The famous Snack Street, with scorpions on a stick and other interesting eats, intersects with it. But most of Wangfujing is dominated by modern malls and Western-branded stores. Just to the west, within walking distance, is the Forbidden City and Tiananmen Square, considered the geographic center of Beijing.

Subway Lines Five and One are nearby and connect to everything a tourist could want. Beijing's subway system is incredible. Thanks to the 2008 Olympics, it has exploded. During the year we are in China, Line Ten is completed and a whole new route, Line Six, opens. Line Seven is under construction. A one-way ticket to any destination is two yuan or about thirty-three cents.

The Foreigners Are in 709

We do a few touristy things the first few days. One of the most memorable is standing in line for two and a half hours in Tiananmen Square in the blazing sun to see Mao. Of course, the line doesn't look that long when we decide to do this. What we learn is that the Chinese, with all their people, are masters of the line. We don't see the line wrapping around the back of the mausoleum and coming back around the front again until we are almost there. Plus, the line is constantly moving, making us believe that getting to the end is possible. And, because everyone must climb stairs to enter, we see people going in. Masters of the line, I tell you.

Vendors appear, selling cheap popsicles, which I think is genius and heaven sent. However, even in the one hundred-plus-degree heat, I tell you they're the worst popsicles I have ever tasted. They taste like salt. Remember, I love ice cream and frozen treats and it's over one hundred degrees, but I still give mine away.

About halfway through the line, I read the sign that says no purses or open shoes. At this point, there is nothing I can do about my sandals and in the end, it isn't an issue. But I do need to ditch my purse. I reluctantly leave my family to find the building across the street with the lockers. The price for storing items is based on the number of cameras included. I've never encountered this basis of deriving cost either before or since.

With only one cell phone, we have no way to communicate, so I just start wandering up and down the line that snakes back and forth, looking for my family. We are reunited after about five minutes to my relief—again, even at fifty, I don't like getting lost or being separated from my family. Plus, they have my passport, which is needed for entry.

We finally make it through security and ascend the steps to the mausoleum and enter the room with Mao's body. He's lying on his back, as you would expect, with a clear cover over him. We aren't allowed to get very close, and security keeps the line moving, but he looks really plastic. Poor guy—he did die in 1976.

During our year in China, the more I learn about Mao, the less I like him. I'm looking forward to the day China buries him in every respect. I think this will be a true symbol of positive change.

Settling into Beijing, July 7 – August 8

School

We're ready to find the girls' school and a home. Jim contacts Our Man in Beijing, Richard Collett, who I imagined to be about sixty and rotund from the sound of his emails. In real life, he's forty-something, tall and slim. What do I know?! Richard sets up the meeting with Beijing Yucai.

The original paperwork from the school stated there would be an entrance exam in order to place the girls. When we meet at the school, the director of the International Department asks Rose and Ella several questions in Chinese, and the girls look at him like deer in headlights. Great! All I'm thinking is—we came all this way and now we're not going to be able to get the girls enrolled in school. I could strangle them.

With some prompting, Rose and Ella do get several words out, and the director covers for them, saying he understands this is an unusual situation for them and this behavior is typical of children. Miracles do happen! Costs are discussed, and the girls are admitted.

This is just before the school gate, where all the students leave their bikes.

This is the entrance to Beijing Yucai. There's a security check point as you go in. The building on the left is the elementary school.

Rose and Ella pose just inside the school in their school uniforms

School is a roller-coaster ride for a good part of the year. Two teachers from the International Department are assigned to serve as our liaisons with Rose's and Ella's teachers and the elementary school. Rose has the most trouble adjusting, but by February she says, "Mom, I hate to admit it, but I actually like school now." Thank you, God.

At times, Rose adamantly refuses to go and stay at school. Not a lot of fun for anyone, and we second-guess our decisions a lot. Many phone calls are made to our friend, neighbor and coincidentally Rose's school counselor, Jen Hanns, who helps us think through some tough decisions.

Jim devises a buddy system for Rose, who is mainly having problems reading the written assignments from the board. With the help of our liaisons, this plan is implemented, and a tutor from the school—Nea—comes to our apartment two to three times per week to help Rose and Ella with homework.

A winter's dinner with Cassie (on the left, our summer tutor) and Nea (on the right)

Nea is one of the sweetest people we'll ever meet. She speaks very little English, so communication with me is minimal. But, since she's tutoring during the dinner hour, she eats with the girls some nights and reciprocates by bringing us dinner or treats other nights.

In addition to extra help in the classroom and the tutor, we also end up bribing Rose to stay in China and go to school. (Read on.) You may not want to follow our parenting technique, but it works for us in the short term. As I like to say, Rose and Ella's psychologist will not be bored with their life stories and how their parents screwed them up. (Parent of the Year again eludes us?)

Beijing Yucai is a public Chinese school. No International or American schools for our immersion experience. Ella's teacher speaks no English, and the teacher Rose ends up with speaks only enough to get very basic information across to me.

The school year starts on Saturday, September 1, 2012. Finding out when the school year ends is quite the challenge along with learning when holiday and vacation days fall—as always, read on. Students are expected to be at school by 7:30 a.m. and picked up by 3:00 p.m.

The school is about a 20 to 30 minute walk. There's no school bus for the girls. So, we walk most days and on occasion catch a cab, which costs five yuan each way (less than a dollar). When we get braver, we figure out the public bus and catch it most mornings and afternoons. It costs less than one yuan (12 cents) for students and two yuan (33 cents) for adults. Special Bus 30 (yes, with the name "Special Bus 30," I feel as if we're on the short school bus for the special-needs kids) is the only city bus on our street and it only runs Monday through Friday during rush hour. So, we have to either walk or catch a cab to pick up the girls in the afternoon.

Catching a cab in Beijing is no easy feat. Late afternoon is especially hard because there is a shift change between three and six—why would you do this during rush hour? So, I discover different walking routes as I learn my way around, and as the year progresses, I prefer the one through the hutong (alley way). This is a vanishing way of life in these alleys, and I like being part of it.

Apartment Hunting and Making A Home

After a few days of seeing the sights in Beijing, we switch hotels to the Holiday Inn Express Temple of Heaven on Nanwei Lu. We do this to be closer to school and to start orienting ourselves to the neighborhood where we'll live. We're also supposed to start apartment hunting at noon.

While the girls and I are out food shopping, I get a call postponing our meeting with the realtors until two, but Jim is at the hotel thinking he needs to get everything moved out of the room and get a taxi. By the time we get to the lobby, Jim is fuming, wondering where we've been. I explain, and we get in a cab.

As usual, the driver has no idea how to get to the Holiday Inn and drives us around longer than needed while he talks to someone on the phone, supposedly getting directions. I'm not very nice and am thinking, "Have you ever heard of a GPS?"

As we are standing in the driveway of the hotel with our baggage around us and the cab is driving off, we start counting our luggage. Guess what? We come up short. The driver conveniently didn't unload our computer. We play the blame game. Again, I have choice thoughts about the driver. We try to trace the cab by video camera from either hotel with no luck. Jim didn't take the receipt. Always take the receipt. So, there's no lead there. Needless to say, the driver doesn't return with our computer.

This loss is a devastating blow to us. Yes, no one was hurt, and we can replace the computer, but this computer was a comfort to us like mac and cheese. Each of us had saved things on it and knew how to use it. It did what we wanted, and we knew where to find things. This computer was like a friend and a connection to home. Plus, replacing it seems like a huge inconvenience I can't even wrap my head around. And, contrary to common belief, electronics aren't cheaper in China; they're more expensive. Just what we need right now is another expense. This adds stress onto the stress of finding housing.

So, after the theft, we now get to look forward to house hunting. Originally, I had illusions of us being on HGTV—International House Hunters—when I imagined us looking for our new home. I'm so glad that didn't happen (not like it was a real possibility) because at one point, I have a total melt-down. Being on TV wouldn't have been pretty.

Let me preface the house hunt with this information. We own and manage rental properties, and some of our tenants never clean. I'm almost positive some don't own vacuums, and things I find in the refrigerators and bathrooms are unmentionable. So, I'm used to dirty, even disgusting. I'll also confess that sometimes the kitchen and bathroom cabinets aren't pristine when new tenants move in, but our rentals are usually freshly painted with new vinyl and carpet. And, we charge about half of what we end up paying for the apartment in China. Plus, I personally have never moved out of or into an apartment or house that is anything but spotless.

So, on our $1,500/month rental budget, I think we can have a nice, fun place with some character in a cool neighborhood—like the French Concession in Shanghai. Our dominating factor in selecting an apartment is proximity to the girls' school. This part of town is not where expats live. It's within the second ring road, which is largely built on the old moat that surrounded the old Beijing city wall. We're talking about a really old area, but unfortunately almost everything has been replaced with nondescript mid-rise buildings among shanties. As the area modernizes, there are some beautiful high-rise apartment buildings, but the area's dirty and a little awkward in its transition. There's nothing kitschy or cute about it.

I wish I'd taken better pictures to illustrate the condition of some of the apartments we were shown. The concept of staging or even cleaning an apartment before showing it hasn't arrived in China yet. The garden apartment may take the prize—yes, they called it a garden apartment, so some marketing is going on.

Here's a glimpse of the "garden" apartment. We go through a grubby hallway to the uninviting brown metal front door. When we open the door, we find they are tearing down a wall to the right so there's brick rubble to negotiate. But when I say to the girls and Jim, "Watch your step!" I mean, don't step in the dog pee.

Despite the dog, no one is living here while it's being renovated. We're told the reno will only take a week—right. They're not changing anything in the antiquated kitchen or bath. It's a small apartment with small rooms.

We have a hard time determining what is what. All I can think is *what a mess* and that everything needs to be cleaned. The apartment is on the first floor, making a garden possible, but when I venture a look out back to the "garden," there's a small walled area with hard-packed dirt, two empty plastic round dish pans, a squash-type plant on a bamboo stake and assorted trash—garden my ...

This is the third or fourth place we've been shown. To top it off, Rose and I have gotten a cold, which includes body aches, and it's ninety-plus degrees outside. Rose is complaining that she's tired and doesn't feel well. Ella is sweating like nobody's business and wants to stop.

We have an entourage of two realtors and two relocation people from Our Man in Beijing who lead us around without telling us where we're going or what we're going to see. I'm a woman who likes some control, especially when it seems those in charge don't know what they're doing, and my children are ready to mutiny. Mind you, this is all being done on foot. No, no big, fancy, leased, air-conditioned car. The realtors are dressed like Mormon missionaries in black ties and pants with white shirts. They have a scooter they take turns riding as we trudge from place to place.

So, at this point, I stop in the middle of the sidewalk and say, "We (the girls and I) are going no farther until we know exactly where we're going, a realistic estimate of time to get there, and I need a promise it isn't going to be another crappy dump." Yes, the ugly American comes out. And guess what, we look at two more dumps. The next day we see two more.

In general, the Chinese don't like public displays of emotion. They basically ignore the situation and act as if nothing happened. It's never acknowledged. It's like I never said anything at all, which infuriates me.
As mentioned, we have moved to the Holiday Inn near the girls' school. However, what I didn't tell you is the two beds in our room are twins. We're all fed up with the sleeping arrangements, and it doesn't look as if any "cute" apartment is going to materialize. It's time to make a decision.

Do we take the apartment a block from the school that has some character but is being replastered and has an old kitchen and bath? It would make a wonderful school commute, and it's only a second-floor walk-up. Or, do we take the apartment that is a thirty-minute walk and has a better bathroom but no bathtub. It's cleaner and has better furniture than anything else we've seen. It's on the seventh floor but with an elevator and is move-in ready.

Did I mention the four of us are sleeping on two small twin beds—if twin beds come in different sizes, which I'm beginning to believe, we got the small ones—and all of us, except Jim, are now sick with flu-like symptoms? We decide on the apartment that's ready. School hasn't started yet, and we'll figure out the commute somehow.

The landlords (husband and wife) are VERY nice, and the husband (Wan) speaks very good English. He completed his master's in Australia. The wife really likes the girls. By the end of our stay, the wife is pregnant with their first child.

Before we move in, they install an additional AC unit (we now have AC in all three bedrooms), provide us with a new washing machine, and install internet. It's a three-bedroom, one-bath apartment. The address is 709, No. 8 Si Ping Yuan, Nan Heng Dong Lu, Xuanwu District, Beijing, China 100053. In two days, we can move in.

In the meantime, we are hit with some unexpected outlays of cash. Unlike in the U.S., where you pay rent monthly, here you pay three months' rent at a time, an additional one month's rent security deposit, yet another month's rent to the realtor and a fee for a full year of internet service at the outset. So, on a very limited budget—our wire transfer hasn't come through, and surprise, surprise, most places don't accept foreign credit cards—we start to buy the necessities—mainly at Wal-Mart (which will take a foreign credit card if you get the right cashier) and Wu-Mart. Yes, the Chinese version of Wal-Mart is Wumart. This sounds like something on *Saturday Night Live,* but it's true.

Since we have a few days before we move in, Jim hires a tutor for the girls and himself from an online site. The expectation is three hours a day Monday through Friday from 9 a.m. to noon at a cost of $12/hour. The tutor meets us at the Holiday Inn for the first time. Her English name is Cassie, which Jim constantly mispronounces. In his defense, we don't know any Cassies back home.

Cassie is from the most Northwestern province in China—Xinjiang Uygur Zizhiqu (above Tibet), and she's Muslim. She explains to us in our first meeting that she is a minority in China. I ask, "How does anyone know you're a minority?" She explains that her hair is more brown than black, the texture of her hair is different, and her eye shape is different. OK. At this point, I can't tell Chinese from Japanese from Vietnamese. So, I'm basically hopeless on this point anyway. And no, I don't think they all look alike, I just can't tell you who comes from where just by facial features.

After tutoring, we walk Cassie toward the subway, but she helps us navigate Wumart, for which I am eternally grateful. Jim and Cassie check out the computers, and the girls and I check out clothes, home goods and food. Cassie will accompany me here several more times as I stock our apartment with essentials such as a water boiler, salt, soy sauce—there are so many kinds, vinegar—again, there are so many kinds, baking soda—for the fridge—etc. Thank you, Cassie. This is the beginning of a very good friendship.

Several days later, Jim ends up buying a new Lenovo laptop at Wumart. But we can't replace the Suzuki piano CDs for the girls or Jim's Chinese CDs that were in the computer case. The Lenovo doesn't have a DVD player, which totally bums us out. No watching the DVDs we brought with us. This further disconnects us from home and creates yet another inconvenience. Also, on the Lenovo, the commands for Word and other programs are in Chinese. Great! Thank goodness for universal icons.

Cassie shows up according to schedule for the next few weeks and, except for missing a few days here and there, until school begins, she's ours. Our routine is for Cassie to tutor as scheduled, and then we go to lunch with Cassie usually joining us. This is a God send, since she introduces us to cuisines from different areas of China. We go to restaurants we never would have ventured into without her. We learn how to order and how to eat different dishes. At one place, if you eat all the noodles in the soup, you get free noodle refills. How great, and who knew?

Rose has the basketball, Ella has the cap on
and Cassie is pictured to the right of me

I'm in my house slippers, which I forgot to change out of. So much for keeping them clean. We're standing in front of our favorite hutong restaurant.

Moving into our place is kind of exciting but a little unsettling for me. The girls are excited because the room they choose for their bedroom is raised about five inches above the rest of the apartment and has curtains instead of a door. They perceive it as a stage, and many original performances ensue.

I'm the least enthusiastic. My expectations have gotten in the way yet again. There's no more hope of finding the trendy, cool apartment. This is home for the year. Great.

The kitchen is typical for China. For appliances, we have two gas burners and a sink. There is a full refrigerator with freezer—in the living room. But everything is dirty; it's not filthy but just not clean. For the entire year, I store no food in the kitchen cabinets just because I can't get the initial picture of the food particles and layer of black filth out of my mind. I store non-perishable food in the never-been-used cupboard in the dining area.

When we open the refrigerator or freezer, it's as if someone with terrible halitosis has yawned and the smell quickly infiltrates the living/dining room area. For the first two months or so, we all shout, "Close the door!" whenever anyone opens the fridge and stands. We continually clean and use lots of baking soda.

The kitchen is equipped with an old heavy-duty wok and an old tea kettle. We use the wok but put the kettle in a cabinet for the duration. I buy an additional pot, mainly to boil pasta, a rice cooker and a water boiler, which get us through the year. It's amazing how little you really need.

Rose is my hero. That little girl scrubs places I can't bear to think about. She gives me the courage to continue and to not complain—as much. She scrubs the fridge and freezer—interior and exterior. She scrubs the exterior of the kitchen cabinets, which have particles of food glued to them. She truly inspires me.

Then, we scrub the tile wall opposite the kitchen counter. At the end of the year, as we are moving out, I will ask myself if the tile wall is two toned. Then, I touch the wall and wipe the black off with my finger. I smile and remember we cleaned only as far as we could reach. Apparently, I have the habit of looking forward and not up.

Jim, who when we agreed on this apartment, promised he would help in every way to get it clean and livable, is now sick with the fever and flu-like symptoms Rose and I had. Of course, during all the cleaning, he is sleeping like a baby only to wake and tell us how sick he is. Thanks, Jim. Ella does a good cleaning job for a while and then gets bored and ornery. She spends most of the time on the sofa watching Chinese cartoons.

Everybody in our little family has their strengths. When times are tough, and you need someone to go the distance, it's Rose. Now, if you're lost, Ella's your go-to person. She's been giving substitute bus drivers directions on the school route since second grade. Jim is our planner. I'm the executor. He plans the trip. I make sure everything's packed. I try to remember this as I restrain myself from wanting to smother him with a pillow as he sleeps and I'm still cleaning on day three.

The above is the exterior of our orange and white twelve-story building. Originally, I thought it was built in the 1970s, but no, it was the '90s. The whole complex forms a rectangle with a parking area in the middle. We live on this front side facing the main street. On the street level, there is a convenience store where Jim will buy his Baijiu (brand of local Chinese liquor—think grain alcohol) and beer (Yan Jing) and the girls and I will buy ice cream. There are two hair salons, a hardware store, a copy shop, a veterinarian, and several more businesses that do things I can't figure out.

We're on the seventh floor. However, to get to our apartment, we take the elevator up to the sixth floor. The elevator stops only on even-numbered floors. We could take the stairs, but I haven't been brave enough yet. OK, I'm a baby. There's nothing wrong with the stairwell except the walls and floor are dirty, it's dingy and dimly lit—think depressing.

Anyway, from the elevator, you go through a gray, dusty, unheated/un-airconditioned corridor—it has a series of windows, which make it bearable—and then, you go up a half flight of stairs to a landing we share with another apartment. As the weeks go by, I come to like the corridor. I like seeing the street scene below and getting a sense of the weather before having to fully embrace it.

An American family livin' the life in China

These two pictures show part of the corridor and Jim opening our front door. Note the small box to the right. That's our milk and yogurt box. Two more small boxes will be added to accommodate our daily order.

In our entire year, we see the people who live across from us less than five times, and we're both startled each time. I never see them long enough to really get a good look at them. They are an older couple who our landlord tells us don't like noise—great. They seem nice enough, but we don't speak the same language and they make no effort to engage us. That's OK.

The bikes in the corridor never move and are covered with dust. We joke that we hope they never move the bike on the left because that's our cue that our landing is next. My friend Jenny says the local joke is that the bikes in the hallway could be new, but in Beijing because of the dust, they look five years old in three days anyway—kind of like our building.

This is Rose answering the front door. Note there are two metal doors—an exterior brown door opening out and a light green one opening in. For a country with practically no crime, especially home break-ins, I find this funny. Why do we need two doors? The exterior one even bolts into the frame.

The Chinese pictures and couplets behind Rose are on the wall when we rent the apartment and remain during our tenure. I have no idea what they say, but it's so Chinese. I like it.

Once you enter the front door (See the tip of the door behind the refrigerator?), the kitchen is to the right. When you step into the open area, the girls' bedroom is to the right, then there's the dining area with fridge and washer, and the entry to the bathroom is next to the washer. The washer will spend the rest of its days in the bathroom.

If you look at the apartment from the girls' room, you see the dining and living room and the entry to the other two bedrooms. Note the big-screen TV in the living room on the photo on the following page.

The Foreigners Are in 709

If you go to the end of the living room, our bedroom is to the left and the bedroom we initially use as an office is straight ahead. As colder weather approaches, we convert the office into the girls' bedroom because the front room gets too cold. One of the radiators is pictured in the living room in the left corner encased in a brown cabinet.

Here's a picture of the back bedroom, which is initially our office. You access the drying porch through the glass doors of this room. The AC is attached to the upper wall. There are two built-in wardrobes facing the desk that aren't pictured.

This picture shows our bedroom. We have a window looking out on the drying porch. We also have three huge mobile wardrobes that aren't shown. You can see our AC unit above the bed.

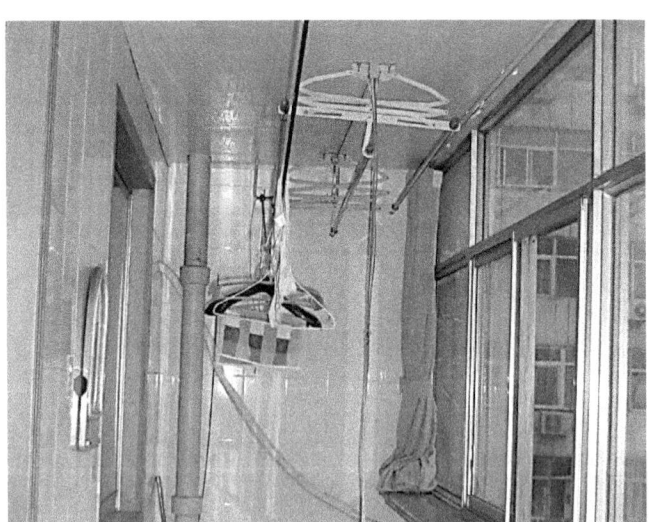

The drying porch

On a blue-sky day, this is the view straight out from the porch. At night, to the left, we can see the lighted kites being flown at Taoranting Park. At night, this view is a little magical. It's breathtaking and fun and so authentically Chinese. At bedtime, during the winter months, the girls and I read in the back bedroom and watch the lighted kites.

The bathroom sink area is separate from the shower and toilet area and isn't shown. In this picture, the shower head is wrapped around the hot and cold-water handle, but it can also be attached to the wall. Above the toilet is the household water heater. Not shown, but just to the left, is where the washer usually sits. There are overhead warming lights we use almost constantly in fall, winter, and spring.

This is probably the cleanest bathroom I will ever have. This setup is great for multitasking. While taking a shower, I usually do a load of laundry, clean the toilet, and hose down the room. The girls and I do long for a hot bath occasionally. A big bonus, when we travel, is a hotel room with a tub.

When I explain our apartment to my friend Jennifer Harper back in the States, she makes everything make sense. She says, "Well, Hope, that's every man's dream—a comfortable sofa, a large-screen TV and a fridge in the living room. Of course, Jim loves it!" You know, she's right.

Helping me to further understand Jim's satisfaction with our apartment, his lack of outrage at the filth of the places we saw while apartment hunting, and his dismissing the necessity to clean our apartment, is a couple I meet at Wumart of all places. As I'm looking for cleaning supplies—of course—I run into Niurka Muerdo and her husband, Lloyd Riggins, who are the only other white people at Wumart—pretty much our entire time in China. We're complete strangers, but we start to talk. They're from the States originally—I'll tell you more about them when I get to the friends section—and I bond with Niurka immediately as she explains Jim's behavior to me.

She asks, "Did you see where he lived before you married him?" I reply, "Yes." She asks, "Was it clean?" To this I reply, "No, I remember thinking I'd never been in a filthier bathroom in all my life, including gas station restrooms."

She says, "See, you have different clean meters." She is so right. I leave feeling so much better. I'm not crazy. The place is filthy by my standards. Jim just has a different meter.

Identity Crisis

On Monday, Cassie finds her way to our new apartment. A new insight sets in as Cassie relays her exchange with the security guard downstairs. As Cassie entered our complex, the guard stopped her and asked where she was going. She replied, "I'm going to tutor some children in Chinese." He stated, "The foreigners are in 709."

Yes, he knows exactly where we live, and our new identity is "The Foreigners." A few weeks later, a little girl visiting her grandmother gets on the elevator with us and asks, "Grandma, you have foreigners in your building?" I know this because my children translate for me and from the looks we get.

This is so strange to me. I've always been the American or maybe when Americans were out of favor in a particular country, I was visiting I'd let people assume I was Canadian. But for the most part, I'm very proud to be an American. Being an American is a big part of who I am. Sometimes it takes leaving America to learn this.

After some thought, I realize being "the foreigners" says more about the Chinese than it does about us. It's how the Chinese see the world: There are the Chinese and then there is everyone else. Most importantly, the two groups are mutually exclusive.

This perspective makes perfect sense when you look at Chinese history. The Chinese were closed off from the outside world for years and before that, foreigners did some horrible things to the Chinese—think Japanese invasions and the Opium Wars just for starters. So, lumping us all together and calling us outsiders is so appropriate. The Chinese word for foreigner—waiguoren—literally means outside-of-the-country person.

But being called an outsider is so... non-inclusive. In America, we take your tired, your poor, your huddled masses …. We're so inclusive—or used to be. I wondered if we would ever be included enough to understand the Chinese people and the things happening around us in any depth.

On the flip side, defining our identity to the Chinese is also somewhat problematic. In the beginning, when Chinese people would ask where we were from, we would get blank stares, which totally confounded us. Charlotte, North Carolina, got no spark of recognition. The U.S., United States of America, America, The States—we tried them all.

At some point, someone finally explained to us that men would understand America because of sports teams and women would understand United States because that's what's taught in school. This seemed to work, and we went with it. But having to grapple with what to call our country, one of the super powers of the modern world, is like Bill Gates having to explain to someone in the U.S. who he is. Who knew?

Not only are we foreigners, but also, we are the only non-Asians in our apartment complex. In fact, we are the only white people for miles in any direction except for isolated pockets of tourists. I never see another white face in our immediate neighborhood the whole year. When walking to drop off or pick up the girls from school, there are sporadic white tourist groups around the Holiday Inn Express Temple of Heaven, mainly in the fall and late spring. Of course, The Forbidden City and Tiananmen Square are only a twenty- minute cab ride away and there are white tourists there. But, if I really want to see white and black people in some quantity, who live in Beijing, I need to go to the northeastern side of Beijing where the expats live, and the embassies are housed.

Regardless of our label, "the foreigners," and being a minority, I feel the Chinese are indifferent to us. In the neighborhood, I think most people know our story. Everyone in our building knows who we are, probably through the security guard or the ladies who run the elevators in our building. Some vendors at the fruit and produce market asked Rose and Ella early on about us, and I know they have passed the word because I have heard them—I do understand a few words and definitely understand gestures and eye movement.

The only person who makes a big deal over us is an old man who's a regular patron at a restaurant with outdoor seating. He sets his beer on the table, waves, and calls out "Waiguoren!" as we pass.

As we're out and about, mainly on the subway, the older Chinese are the most curious about us. They approach the girls. They ask the same questions pretty much in the same sequence each time. Here's the dialogue when I'm with them: The Chinese person looks at me and asks the girls in Chinese, "Is that your teacher?" The girls answer, "No, that's our mother." Then: "Is your father Chinese?" "No, our father's American, too." Silence. You can practically hear the wheels turning in their heads as they try to figure this out. I say, "Girls, explain." They relent and say, "We're adopted. We were born in China but live in America now." The Chinese person then leans in and asks, "Are your parents good to you"? What will they say this time? goes through my head. "Yes, they're good to us," is the response. The Chinese then say what good people we are. The girls grow very bored with this exchange, but the Chinese are so earnest with their questions, I love it.

As a side note, adoption is still a strange concept to the Chinese. I'm told several adoption stories involving Chinese families, but none of them have happy endings. I can't prove this, but I sense the majority of Chinese people wonder why anyone would adopt.

Back on topic—it doesn't bother me that I'm a minority. I kind of like it. For once, the physical characteristics I have been most self-conscious about all my life, my curly hair and almost anemic white skin, are sought after in this society. How great is that?

Setting Up the Household

Cassie helps me source household items and supplies. She sets up our bottled water service with a little store in the hutong. After tasting several brands, we settle on the one Cassie likes because I can't tell any difference. FYI—you can't drink water from the faucet in China unless you boil it first. I even boil the water I use to rinse our clean dishes.

With our purchase of thirty tickets, we get a dispenser and the delivery of bottled water to our apartment thirty times. The dispenser can be plugged in, and we can have hot water as well as room-temperature. Whenever we need a refill, the girls or Jim call the business and within half an hour someone comes with a large bottle of water on their shoulder and takes the empty. This works great, but I have to plan ahead. Only once, with written notes in front of me, do I call for a refill because my Chinese is so limited. This supply of tickets lasts us the whole year.

In America, I've seen immigrant parents come with their elementary-school-aged children to my husband's office to have their taxes prepared. The children translate whatever Jim says to their parents and vice versa. The parents are totally dependent on their children for this adult task. That's the way I am now in many situations.

In general, I think most people who know me would describe me as independent. However, I now know the frustration and to some degree the shame, of having to rely on my children because I haven't learned the language. When out on my own, I sometimes just hold out my coins in my open hand and let the vendors take what is needed. Is this not like being five years old again? I have mixed emotions about this.

Cassie also arranges for our milk to be delivered. Each morning, seven days a week, we get little containers of milk and yogurt delivered to the little boxes outside our door. It's not cheap, but it's delicious and it saves us from lugging milk back to the apartment. As the year progresses, Rose and Ella are able to write notes to the milkman to change our order and to stop and restart delivery when we travel. The bill comes monthly in the milk box, and I pay by putting the cash payment in the box.

Cake and milk

Next, Cassie helps us with our wire transfer. After ten days of checking our account twice daily and not seeing our balance change, I call NCBT (now, South State Bank), where we bank. Side note: I strongly recommend banking with a small bank. All I have to do is call Brian or Monica's direct line. Yes, two people whom I know and who know me. They understand our situation and solve our money problems during phone conversations. This is truly priceless.

In this instance, Brian checks and says the wire has gone through, so the problem must be something on China's end. So, Cassie takes me to Bank of China, where we opened an account with the help of our relocation people. FYI: Bank of China is the best bank for foreigners because money transfers are supposed to be the easiest through them. What we discover is that our money has been sitting in our Chinese account for days. However, it's in U.S. dollars, not in Chinese RMB (yuan), so it doesn't show up on the ATM. Quickly, we convert to yuan and have money again. Hurray!

Now that we have funds, it's back to making household purchases. Whenever I ask Cassie where I should buy something, I shake my head, smile, and wish I could retract my words because I know she's going to say, "Online." She helps me order food—mainly rice and cereal—and household items such as mattress pads, sheets, knives, and a rice cooker online. It's not an easy process because sites such as Tmall don't accept American credit cards, you must be a member, and it's all in Chinese. But over the course of the year, we order many things online with Ella understanding enough about Tmall and Chinese that she can help me when Cassie isn't around.

Above, in front of the stove, are Ella with the new rice cooker and Rose with rice

This picture is of my new Fuanna sheets. I order them because I love the colors (the dragon is hot pink, lime and moss green and gold) and  the design—and because I'm so hungry for something truly nice. I really wanted fitted bottom sheets, but the Chinese don't use or sell them.

Cassie later explains that the sheets I chose have what is considered the traditional Chinese matrimonial motif. The dragon represents the male, and the phoenix represents the female. This pattern is usually given to newlyweds. Wow, I learned something, and I still like the sheets. Among the household things I really miss and I can't find at all or can't find easily are paper towels, sponges, and fitted sheets.

I discover through *The Beijinger*—an English magazine catering to expats—that there is an IKEA in Beijing. I'm so excited I can hardly stand it. Cassie, her sister, Bali, Rose, and I pay a visit. I find this incredible. It's exactly like the IKEA store we shop at in Charlotte right down to the menu, location, and layout.

The one unusual thing is that the Chinese take naps on the display beds. It's so bizarre. And, they don't remake the beds. Every bed is either being slept in or is disheveled. You can Google this if you don't believe me.

I buy four matching chairs for our dining room table, two floor lamps, plates, colorful plastic cups, and a plant holder to put chopsticks in. Yes, no table knives or forks for us for the whole year. Usually, I don't like to assemble things, but in this instance, I'm grateful that the larger items come in pieces. I read on the IKEA site that I can have all this delivered, but we decide we can fit ourselves and our goods in a taxi for the same price as the delivery and I'll have them in the apartment today. I'm elated.

Cassie is the first one to make a real meal in our kitchen. She and her sisters will make other meals for us. On this occasion, she teaches us how to make tomato sauce and cook potatoes in the wok.

Here's an obscure Cassie fact that we find very amusing: Cassie's grandmother owns a camel. How many people can say that? Apparently, camel milk is especially good for you. Cassie says it's the closest thing to human mothers' milk. However, we're a little disappointed to learn that Cassie's grandmother doesn't ride the camel.

Taoranting Park, Beijing Zoo, And the Flood

This is our neighborhood park—Taoranting. The closest entrance to our apartment is just through the hutong and to the left. It's a beautiful, large park. There's a lake with paddle and electric boats in fun shapes and sizes, tons of weeping willows, beautiful bridges, pagodas, lots of refreshment and souvenir stands, runners, musicians, and older people playing board games, dancing, and practicing tai chi. It's a very active yet peaceful, fun place to be. And, on this particular Sunday, it's just glorious with an amazing blue sky. Can you tell I miss consecutive days of blue sky? It seems to be gray or rainy for five days, and then we get one clear, beautiful day. I just want to soak it up when the sky is blue.

Here's a map and some pictures of the park. Most of these were taken in October during the Moon Festival celebration. The park was decorated in elaborate displays of flowers, special craft booths appeared along with new food vendors, and dancing and singing performances. It was truly amazing to be part of this.

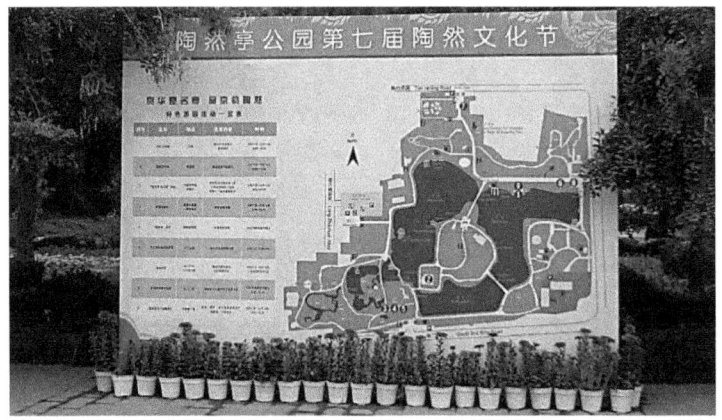

Ella, Rose and me in a photo-op area

Ribbon dancers

Rose and Ella making and painting a kite

Red lanterns hung from the trees

A floral dragon by the pond

An American family livin' the life in China

Craftsman

A man with calligraphy brushes that use water instead of ink to write on the sidewalks

The Foreigners Are in 709

We go to the zoo today—July 22, 2012. Our apartment is a couple of blocks from subway Line Four, so it takes us about twelve minutes to walk there. The stop we use most often is Taoranting, but we can also use the Caishikou stop near Wal-Mart. Line Four is a fairly new addition to the Beijing subway system. It's nice and clean, and today it's really convenient because the line has a stop for the zoo. The zoo is a great bargain—it's free except you pay five yuan (less than $1/person) to see the pandas.

The pandas we see inside are eating bamboo. The pandas outside are doing NOTHING—it's so hot. They're the smart ones. The zoo is not a must-see. The animals don't seem to be well cared for. The black bears are in a concrete pit with trash and an enormous accumulation of plastic water bottles littered around them. Even though there is a sign saying not to feed the bears, people keep throwing food and other things down to them. This makes me sad, but it's a gorgeous day—another blue-sky day.

For the two previous days, we had gray skies, and yesterday it poured with thunder and lightning lasting for hours. We later find out …

> *In a twenty-hour period on July 21, 2012, a flash flood hit the city of Beijing in the People's Republic of China. Within a day of the flooding, 56,933 people were evacuated, and 79 people were killed. In addition, the floodwaters caused at least $1.6 billion (U.S) in damages and destroyed at least 8,200 homes. In the city, more*

than 1.6 million people were affected by the flood overall.

Fangshan District was the most heavily affected area of Beijing, located in the southwest, which received a record-setting 18 inches of rain, the highest recorded since 1951. The Juma River flooded its banks and reached a flow rate of 88,000 cubic feet per second. A woman in Fangshan reported the river rose 1.3 meters in her home in approximately ten minutes.

At Beijing Capital International Airport, the floods resulted in the cancellation of over 500 flights, stranding 80,000 travelers.

This is a bit of the blurb from the internet. It's a little scary to me. Although Beijing is huge (think sprawling like Houston), and the area where the deaths happened is at the foot of the mountains nowhere near where we live, it does make me pause and wonder whether anyone would have looked after us because ... we are totally clueless. We get one English TV channel with no local news. We don't understand the Chinese news channels, and forget about Chinese radio or newspapers. The internet and calls from friends at home who have heard Beijing news are our best sources.

When attempting to get a cab that morning to no avail, we do notice that the street in front of our apartment is flooded, so we abandon our plans for the day and opt for staying in and watching TV. The girls like to watch a Chinese cartoon, *Xi Yang Yang*, and Jim will watch Chinese war movies. I watch the English Channel on occasion.

The only damage we incur from the flood is the soggy cardboard pizza delivery boxes. The delivery guy is soaked. Can you image delivering pizza on a motor scooter during a flood? Thank you, Pizza Hut. Oh, and remember, you don't tip in China. So, this poor guy is delivering pizza to dumb Americans who have no idea how bad it is on the streets, and he gets nothing additional for his trouble. Months later when we try to order pizza again, they have taken our area off the delivery map. Guess I know why.

Rose's 11th Birthday and The Summer Palace

Here's the princess—for a day—with her castle in the background.

Remember, I'm a birthday person. I think your birthday is the most special day of the year and the people you love need to celebrate that you're in this world. Bottom line, I want my family's birthdays to be special, and everything must go right on that day. Of course, this just leads to everything going wrong.

We have several surprises for Rose's birthday ... the purple tent we ordered online for her bed turns out to be pink. The heart-shaped cake with the smooth chocolate icing and raspberries on top, which we ordered days ago, is round with chocolate shavings. When we inquire at Wumart why we didn't get the cake still displayed in the case, we are simply told—"We can't make that one." Nice to know.

The special candle for Rose's cake that I bought in Hefei (where Rose was adopted) is supposed to open into a lotus flower and play *Happy Birthday*. It's the same kind she had on her first birthday cake. With that one, we finally put the candle outside because it wouldn't shut off. How many times can you listen to *Happy Birthday*? This time, the candle plays correctly but never opens. It has a meltdown. Literally, it just melts—plastic and all.

The rest of the day we have nice surprises. Our plan is to tour the Summer Palace. It is VERY convenient for us. It's also on subway Line Four and is the second to last stop. The entry fee is $5 (30 yuan) for adults and half price for the kids. So, for $15 we have a wonderful afternoon.

On the subway, I make eye contact with other foreigners. We follow them and proceed to spend the whole afternoon together. Manuel, Marta and Kayveen. (I think his name is Kevin, but this is how everyone pronounces it, including us.) All of them speak very good English, but because two of them are from Spain and Kayveen is Chinese, accents do add some comedy. Along with Kayveen being Kevin, Manuel is talking to us about the "bitch" which we figure out from context clues is not Marta but actually the word "beach".

Our three new friends are great company and solve a mystery for us. We've wanted to rent a paddle boat at Taoranting Park so badly but have refused because of the price. We've been wondering how anyone can afford it. When we attempt to pay, the boat rental person wants the equivalent of $50, but the sign says $10 per hour. I wonder if there's a five-hour minimum. Jim and Ella make numerous attempts to rent a boat for $10.

Well, we rent a boat to ride around the lake at the Summer Palace with our friends for 300 yuan or $50 and are elated to discover that $50 is a deposit and it IS only $10 an hour. We foresee many more boat rides in our future. All in all, Rose has a nice, memorable eleventh birthday.

Restaurants and Food

The pictures on the following pages show our favorite neighborhood restaurant. The chef is leaning out the window in the first one. If most of you looked in that window, you wouldn't go in. The restaurant itself isn't that clean, but the food is excellent, and bottom line, it's convenient and we haven't gotten sick yet. We later discover they have carry-out and order from there at least once a week.

Some interesting things happen in local Chinese restaurants—smoking is allowed, men go shirtless, napkins are scarce, but toothpicks are plentiful, plates are chipped and wet. And watch out for split-pants babies. One day we eat lunch at DQ—yes Dairy Queen (it's next to Wal-Mart and is exactly the same as home) a little boy with split pants is seated next to me. When the next people come to sit down, there is some hesitation—the seat is wet. Yes, the little boy had peed in the chair.

Let's set the record straight. Chinese food is amazing. There are more wonderful sauces and dishes than most people could name. Every province and region and many of the towns and cities have their own distinct dishes with complementary sauces and seasonings.

Some food preparation is a craft. One of the most interesting and different food creations we see in China is watching pasta being made. You should ask for a Shanxi restaurant, where Shanxi noodles are being made. It's nothing like you've ever seen or imagined. No machines, no knives; it's all stretched and divided by hand in seconds. It's no wonder Marco Polo took pasta back to Italy. It even beats watching dumplings being made, which is pretty amazing.

On some tourist streets, you will see a taffy-like candy being stretched from a wooden pole, small animal shapes being blown like glass from hot caramel-colored goo, and Chinese zodiac animals being made from caramelized sugar. These are true crafts.

However, as mentioned before, the Chinese eat creatures and parts of creatures that Americans these days usually don't eat—eyes, feet, hooves, intestines, donkey, and jellyfish, to name a few. Not that there is anything wrong with this. In fact, I reiterate that these may be more nutritious than what we eat. And, looking back, I think when they first arrived in America, our ancestors ate similarly. But as we have become more affluent, we waste, and prefer only the best cuts from the best livestock.

All this being said, reading the menu translations can be great mealtime entertainment. Here's a sampling of entrees from a menu the other day—Fragrant Chicken Gristle, Sautéed Egg with Black Fungus, and if you want another fungus, try the Blended Black Fungus. You could have Marinated Gizzards, Ox Tendon with Flavor (I hate the ones without flavor—don't you?), or Braised Ass Meat Sichuan Style. You choose.

Then, on the other hand, there are some things you shouldn't eat. Because of environmental conditions in China, infectious disease, and inadequate safety standards, you need to avoid some foods from time to time. While we are in China, about twenty percent of the lamb skewers sold on the street are actually cat. Some are soaked in lamb urine to make them taste more like lamb. No joke, we read this in *The Beijinger* after we have consumed them on a weekly basis for about six months. I'm so mad because they're an easy meal for me to pick up and were a "healthy," easy snack. Our favorite place to purchase them was next to Taoranting Park, which has lots of cats. I often wonder if this was a good thing or a bad thing.

What?

Another piece of news *The Beijinger* shares is that some restaurants use cooking oil siphoned from in-ground grease traps and resold. Yuck! While we're there, there is a bird flu epidemic scare. This cuts all poultry and eggs from our diet for several months. Also, ginger is said to be contaminated with ground chemicals. I try not to be rude or a health fanatic, but if the locals tell me things or I read it in a reliable source, I listen.

The following pictures show a street restaurant in the hutong just a block from our apartment. We send the girls there to buy breakfast for us a lot. One thing we don't carry out from there is soup. They put their carry-out soup in plastic bags, which I find very unappetizing. I'm sorry, but it looks as if someone threw up in the bag. But the dumplings (baozi) and fried bread (youtiao) are great. We also grab breakfast many mornings on the way to school from a street stall. The fried eggs sandwiched between a sesame biscuit, which we watch them make, are so delicious, fresh, and cheap.

Take-out dumplings in plastic bags are fine, but not soup

The one meal we all love is Beijing Hot Pot. It's water-based like the individual hot pot we had in Shanghai, but it has this amazing sesame sauce. Here's a picture of the pot.

Coal in the center cone provides the heat. The seasonings have already been added to the boiling water.

This sauce is the defining ingredient. There are many hot pot variations in China, but this sesame sauce is the magic ingredient of Beijing hot pot. You dip all cooked food in it, and it tastes wonderful.

These pictures are taken at the restaurant we frequent. It's a Muslim restaurant called JuBaoYuan, on Niu Jie (literally, Ox Street) about a twenty- to thirty-minute walk from our apartment. We try other Beijing hot pot restaurants in the neighborhood, but the sauce, shao bing (bread—see the picture below), and the quality of the meats are best here. Our friends Jenny and Simon originally introduce us to this restaurant. They teach us how to order and cook the food. One word of caution, before you try any hot pot, you need to master chop sticks, so you don't get burned.

The Foreigners Are in 709

Beef and lamb are the meats shown. Each person gets an individual sesame sauce, and you add as much cilantro and onion as you like. There's also sweetened garlic. None of us like the garlic, and we finally figure out how to not order it. The dish pictured just above the sauce contains the mushrooms, garlic, ginger, and other ingredients to season the boiling water.

This is shao bing, a dark bread that has a curry taste and is covered with sesame seeds. It's warm, fresh, and delicious. This restaurant has the best.

Jenny, Simon, Jim, and Ella cooking

Check Out This Menu

Some days nothing is noteworthy. Let's face it, in life, most days aren't that memorable even when you're traveling. But, if you take the sum of the parts, sometimes things are just funny. Here's an example.

For some time, we have wanted to try this little bakery restaurant on Taoranting, a couple of blocks from the subway station. The restaurant is always crowded, which is one of our big clues that it must be good. So, we go in and order at the counter. Remember going to Chinese restaurants and ordering items from column A, B, and C? Well, here you have three columns—Cantonese Snacks,

Cantonese Claypot, and Cantonese Claypot Gruel. Any takers on the gruel?

We look around at what others are eating. I don't know which column this falls under, but we point to someone's pasta dish and that's what we all have—pasta gruel?

Even before we enter the restaurant, we're thinking maybe a nice, tasty pastry might be good for dessert. After all, we're at a bakery.

Inside, we notice the fly swatters hanging in front of the posters on either end of the pastry display. Then we notice the flies. The pastries aren't looking so tasty anymore. Maybe those aren't raisins?

And last but not least ...

So, we're filling up on pasta because we're not having dessert. We're watching the world go by from our window table when a little boy stops in front of us, looks around and pees. Public restrooms are abundant, and you never see little girls peeing, but little boys seem to be everywhere. Anyway, the sequence of events today just makes us shake our heads and laugh out loud. So much for an appetizing meal.

First Visa Trip: Taiwan

We were so excited to be able to get a one-year tourist visa for our China trip. We'd thought we could only get one for six months. Then, when we arrive in mainland China and discover with our one-year tourist visa we must leave mainland China every sixty days, we are pretty bummed. We hadn't anticipated this additional expense and the inconvenience.

In all fairness, we had seen the sixty days on the visa but thought it couldn't possibly be enforced. Make no mistake about it; it is enforced with a vengeance. But now, after settling into Beijing and making the decision to go to Taiwan, we're warming to the idea of leaving every sixty days.

We barely scratch the surface, but we love what we see of Taiwan. We fly into Taipei by way of Hong Kong. Yes, we fly past Taiwan, but remember, this extra travel is an unexpected expense and this route saves us $200. And … we have the time.

In Taipei, we stay at the Charming Castle Hotel in the Old Town Center. Initially, when Jim tells me the name of the hotel, I find it a bit suspect, thinking that "charming" is very subjective. The hotel does turn out to be a good kind of charming with lots of moldings, insets and an interesting (in a good way) bathroom, and the woman at the front desk is immensely helpful. Breakfast is included with the room, and they don't quibble about the kids. It isn't the best location as far as being able to easily walk to tourist destinations or the subway, but it's nice, clean and upscale.

As a side note, it's 30 TWD (New Taiwan Dollar) to a U.S. dollar. So, you carry around all these $1,000 bills. It's kind of fun.

The first day we head to the National Palace Museum, which everyone raves about. To be honest, I've gone to some museums I really like, but most are boring. Some, I just like the gift shops—sorry MOMA. And, when you go with children who are constantly telling you how bored they are and how boring everything else is, it can be unbearable. Knowing all of this, I tell you the National Palace Museum *should* be raved about.

By dumb luck, the taxi lets us off on the lowest level by the children's museum. We enter and are all totally engaged. The children's section introduces us to the highlights of the museum, which gives us things to look for in the actual museum and makes us feel knowledgeable. Plus, the woman running the exhibit plans the rest of our tour for us.

She tells us to go to the jewelry exhibit—Royal Style: Qing Dynasty and Western Court Jewelry. Much of the Western jewelry is from Cartier. The exhibit explains how during the early 1900s when an affluent middle class was growing and industrialists in the West had more money than the royals, the part jewelry played in showing status. There's a tiara that belonged to Doris Duke. In Charlotte, we live around the corner from the Duke Mansion, so this makes us a little giddy. Then the woman suggests we come back to the main museum and eat lunch at the fourth-floor restaurant (we would have never found this restaurant on our own because the first elevator we take only goes to the third floor and there is a nice sandwich shop on the main level), and then go on the English tour of the main museum at 3:00. We sign up for it immediately.

I highly suggest the children's area even if you don't have children. It's well done, and you learn so much. The restaurant on the fourth floor is expensive, but the view is great. By the end of the English guided tour, the kids are bored and tired—well, we all are after five hours—but it's a wonderful experience.

From the museum, we take a taxi to the trendy neon section of town—Ximending. There are tons of twenty-somethings, multi-story hairstyling salons, clothes shops, and tattoo parlors. We finally find the Thai restaurant recommended in the *Lonely Planet* guide book—it's OK, but the highlight is meeting three women from Hawaii who have been living in Taiwan for the last seven years teaching English. They give us tips on what to do the next day.

Following the ladies' suggestions, the next day we take the subway to the Maokong Gondola, which is by the zoo. It's drizzling, and the gondola is closed. We're bummed, but we take a bus to the top, which surprisingly is quite scenic and fun.

Per our guidebook, we go to the Yuan Xu Yuan teahouse, where we get a private room. We sit on pillows on the floor, look at tremendous views of Taipei (after the clouds clear), eat interesting food, and drink local tea. The waitress helps us make the tea—who knew it could be so complicated—and explains how to eat the food. Do we sound like the Beverly Hillbillies yet?

Ella is holding one of the floor seat cushions

Well, when we get the bill, we are quite surprised. Instead of it being $40 as we expect, it's $80. We should have asked the waitress to explain this, too, but we were there for two hours and the gondola is running now. We want to catch it before more rain comes and they shut it down again. So, we chalk it up as an experience and move on.

Ella, who is all excited about the gondola ride, is a little less excited when she gets on and sees how high we are. It's also a long ride with several stops, which doesn't delight Ella either. What can I say? Consoling a crying child does wonders for your own fear of heights.

The next morning we take the train to Hualien which takes

about four hours. Unfortunately, Jim couldn't book these train tickets from Beijing. We couldn't even find an English guidebook of Taiwan in Beijing—does this say something of the relationship between the two countries? So, when we go to the train station in Taipei the day before our planned train trip, there are no more seats on the train there or back. So, we buy standing tickets.

The woman at the information center really likes the girls and thinks standing will be too much for them. She suggests we get on either the first or last car and look for vacant seats. We will use this advice on other trains as well.

On the way there, we find a large open space at the back of the first car where the girls and I sit on the suitcase, eat snacks, look out the window, play on the iPad, and generally have a good time. Jim finds a seat from time to time, sits on the floor at times, and is basically content. Piece of cake.

On the way back, we aren't so lucky and get to hang out, leaning against the suitcase or a wall by the handicapped bathroom. There are about twelve others crammed in with us. At times, it's entertaining because three little boys keep coming back and opening the bathroom door on people. Rose and Ella are excellent sports and don't complain once.

Once in Hualien, we take a taxi to Taroko National Park. Jim has read about what to do in the guidebook and also got info from our friend Ken in Charlotte. So, for $50 we hire a taxi to take us to a restaurant for lunch (every recommended restaurant in the guidebook has gone out of business), with a stop at the information center and two short hikes before it takes us to our hotel in the park—the Silks Place Hotel, which is a great hotel.

One hike is a little scary. There was a typhoon the week before our trip that severely damaged the roads and makes us think twice about how safe and stable the trails are. Hard hats are standard issue at any time, and when you see the boulders at the bottom of the gorge, it makes you wonder why anyone would take this risk. Because it's so beautiful, and what are the chances—right?

For those of us who don't like heights too much and are a teeny, tiny bit claustrophobic, the Lishui Trail offers sections that will challenge a bit of both. Parts of this hike are on the edge of the mountain where you can clearly see the ground is cracking and water is coming down (yes, making it more unstable), and then there's a dark tunnel. There is no way around the tunnel. I check. At certain places, such as this juncture with the tunnel, we just feel stuck. We don't want to go forward but, then again, we don't want to go back. Adding to the stress, Jim has forgotten to bring the "torch". Can he not remember anything?

What makes the hike bearable is good signage. The sign before the tunnel clearly states that the tunnel is thirty meters and makes a right-angle turn, where we will again see light. It also suggests you bring a torch—I'm sure it translates to flashlight, but torch makes me laugh which somewhat relieves my anxiety. I mean, doesn't everyone carry a torch? Anyway, we're alive to tell about it. Our cab driver does come looking for us.

A picture looking back at the hotel as I hike

The hotel is wonderful—very spa-like and definitely caters to English-speaking clientele. First off, Jim and the girls go for a swim in the rooftop infinity pool overlooking the gorge. The pool area is spectacular. The views and the amenities are worth the expense alone. While in the hot tub, they make a new friend who is part owner of a restaurant in Beijing—we will later drop his name at Temple Restaurant Beijing and have several wonderful, expensive meals there, including Mother's Day 2013.

I go listen to a Guzheng performance in the lobby. This instrument is like a small, horizontal harp. Afterward, the very nice performer tries to explain to me how to play it. I try to explain I'm tone deaf and musically impaired but, with her help, the instrument sounds beautiful as I pluck one string. After dinner, we all go to the Aboriginal dance performance also at the hotel.

The next morning we eat a wonderful buffet breakfast. The girls love that the restaurant has a real honey comb dripping honey for their toast. Jim loves the chocolate croissants. I love it all.

Jim and the girls again enjoy the outdoor pool—our suntan lotion was confiscated at the airport, and Jim now has a horrendous sunburn.

I hike a very safe, scenic trail with a view of a beautiful temple next to the hotel that I enjoy so much I insist the girls join me on a second climb. Jim continues to burn by the pool.

One other note: As Jim was booking our hotel reservation online for the Silks Place Hotel, the Expedia price was $230/night, and the price on Agoda.com when booking in English was $200, but since he was tenacious and booked it in Chinese, we got it for $165. Go, Jim! This is why I forgive him for not remembering the torch.

Exploring and making a life in Beijing, August 13 – October 13

Famous Beijing Sights

Back in Beijing with only a few weeks before school starts, my mission is to show the girls as much of the city as possible. Jim stays home and works—someone needs to finance our excursions. Plus, he isn't as big a tourist as I am. This becomes more apparent in our last few months in Beijing, but I continue to try to share things with him. He just doesn't know how lucky he is.

Olympic Village

Above, the girls are pictured in front of the Bird's Nest, where the 2008 Olympic Games opening ceremony, as well as other competitions, took place. The interior is not accessible when we're there. But the exterior is amazing, as is the exterior of the Water Cube, which is across the walkway.

The sheer size of the Olympic Park is almost overwhelming. To quote from the brochure—The Olympic Park housed forty-four percent of the venues. It's the largest group of Olympic venues in the history of the Olympics, covering 11.59 square kilometers. This is about 4 and a half square miles.

Beijing does a great job of making the park easily accessible. You take subway Line Eight to the Olympic Sports Center stop and here you are. There are tons of vendors—note Ella's umbrella in the Cube picture. There are tons of people, and there's a ton to see. The girls go to a science museum here on a school trip that Ella talks about for months.

Rose and Ella are standing in front of The Water Cube

It now houses a water park in addition to swimming events. At the end of our stay, we pay to enjoy the water park, which ends up being one of the girls' favorite things about China. Jim is not so enthused. He thinks it's expensive and the restroom changing area should be a lot nicer and cleaner. I sit upstairs where I can view everything and eat. Maybe this is why Jim doesn't like to tour with me?

Bugs on a skewer

During our August excursion, we also visit the Olympic food court. Our meal here isn't very good, but seeing the scorpions and other creatures on sticks makes it worthwhile. You'll see most of these same critters being sold on Snack Street just off Wangfujing, so don't worry if you miss it here.

Rose and Ella are pictured with freshly made edible Chinese zodiac animals made from caramelized sugar—I think. The person takes the hot caramel-colored goo, draws the animals on a marble slab, and then places a stick across it. It's amazing to watch.

An American family livin' the life in China

Caramel Chinese zodiac snacks

Another day we visit 798 Art District, which is a cool, artsy place on the upper east side of Beijing—I'm excited to finally find a cool area in the city. But at first, I'm not sure. It's an old electronics factory that supposedly has been converted. When the taxi drops us off, it's looking pretty bleak, but after a block or two, we look down an alley and see restaurants, bars, shops, and galleries.

Without a car in a totally new area to us, getting to the 798 Art District is a bit scary. The trip takes us nearly an hour on the subway. Then, the subway stop we want is closed (this has NEVER happened to us before), so we get off at the next stop. No one else gets off—strange. We're already thrown off, and this stop is like a portal to a different planet.

The Foreigners Are in 709

We emerge from the subway hallways devoid of people—this is China … there are always people—to a bike lot with only a couple of bikes, no people and no road in sight. I'm thinking we have gone down the rabbit hole and my name is Alice. We quickly, and with a little panic, go back down to the subway, which again is empty, except we find two workers—thank God. We explain that we need a taxi, and they show us the other exit where there is a road. Fortunately, a taxi comes rather quickly. Rose and Ella give the driver directions in Chinese, and we are dropped off at a deserted edge of the district.

By this time, we just need food and drinks. We quickly find a rather eclectic restaurant and feast on curry chicken and rice, a rice and egg dish served in a small wooden barrel, and I have pasta with tomato and meat sauce. The meal is good and priced very reasonably. Sometimes you go to places expats like and you pay high American restaurant prices—not here.

We look around a little and decide we definitely will come back—we never do, unfortunately. It's too hard for me to navigate coming here by subway and taxi. I have to commend Rose and Ella for doing a grand job of directing the taxi back to the correct subway stop. In route, we spot IKEA, which becomes our excursion the next Sunday.

The girls are now in school, and the weather is a bit more pleasant for touring. So, this weekend the whole Young family is together visiting one of the most famous tour sites in the world—The Forbidden City.

Above, we are standing where the emperors in the Ming and Qing Dynasties would have entered on the marble bridge over the Inner Golden Water River, in front of the south gate of the Forbidden City. I love the fancy names.

The Forbidden City is literally the geographic center of Beijing, across the street from Tiananmen Square. We go by it all the time. Jim and I toured the Forbidden City with our adoption group before Rose's adoption in July 2002.

Over the years, we have laughed at what has become an iconic line from John, the Chicago lawyer in the group, who said, "I know why it's called the Forbidden City ... Because it's so f----g hot!" No truer words have been spoken. Why do you think the Chinese royal families went to the Summer Palace for the summer? You may have wondered why we put this big, easily accessible attraction off until now—September. Now you know.

The tickets are very affordable—$10 for adults and $3 for students. No need for us to pay for a guide or headsets. I bought the "Revised and Updated English Tour Guiding in Beijing" book the last time I was at the Foreign Language Book Store on Wangfujing Street, so I conduct our tour. Adding to my credentials, Cassie tells me this is the book the Chinese use to study to become certified English guides.

It takes us a little over two hours to see most of The Forbidden City, and to my credit; we pretty much know what we're looking at the whole time. I love this book.

To quote a little from the book: The Forbidden City is the former Imperial Palace for the Ming and Qing Dynasties. Twenty-four emperors lived there over a span of 491 years (1420 to 1911). It's the largest palatial structure and the largest piece of ancient Chinese architecture in existence today in the world. It's a must-see.

Yes, The Young Family Adopts Another Girl

What do the Youngs do in China? Adopt. Yes, we've adopted two daughters from China, but this time it's a Chinese kitten. Her name is TaoTao.

Something definitely got lost in translation. I thought we were going to FOSTER a cat. You know, take wonderful care of one and then give it back.

An American family livin' the life in China

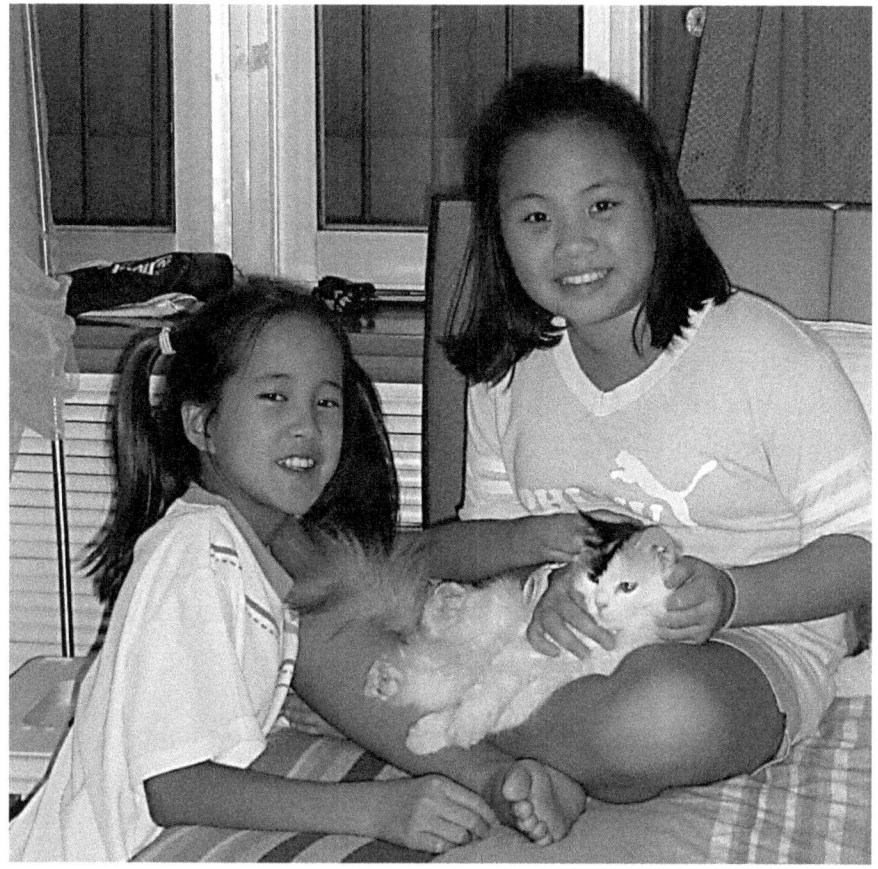

Rose, Ella, and TaoTao—three months old

Here's the story—It starts as a bribe to get Rose to go to school. Yes, yet again the elusive Mother of the Year award eludes me. And, yes, we stooped to "What do you want that will get you to go to school?" (Bad parents?)

Anyway, on the other side of the kitten story, is Judy (her English name). Judy found TaoTao on the street near her house when she was only a few weeks old and took her in to live along with her white rabbit. As TaoTao grew, the rabbit liked TaoTao less and less. Judy came to the realization that one of them had to go. As she tells it, "TaoTao is the cuter one of the two and has a better chance of being adopted." Yeah, right. Is thinking a rabbit and a cat are going to cohabit not a sign that the Chinese know nothing about cats?

Then, Jim and the girls happen on the ICVSasia.com website, where TaoTao's picture is posted, and Rose has to have TaoTao. By the time we meet TaoTao, we HAVE to have the kitten and of course, it isn't for fostering.
So, as we're sitting in Judy's apartment with this kitten, who is a half-grown cat with long hair (I'm thinking we have a dog that doesn't shed for a reason), I ask what TaoTao means in English. Guess … just guess. Of course, it couldn't mean cutie or sweet thing. No, no, TaoTao means naughty. Yes, we get the naughty kitty.

To add to my misgivings, Jim has discovered that rabies kills more people in China than any other infectious disease including AIDS, the flu, etc. Rabies is a big problem here. So, since TaoTao is a stray, we take her straight to the vet for shots. Literally, we take the cat, which Judy has placed in a bird cage, from Judy's apartment directly to the vet's office. If you think the birdcage carrier is weird, Judy originally wanted to give us TaoTao in a plastic grocery bag. Even I thought that was a bad idea.

In the next few days, we take ourselves to a doctor to consult about rabies vaccines for us. Long story short, only Ella has to get the shots. (Our family experience with rabies could be material for a short story.) Our free kitten has now cost us $700 in less than a week.

On the positive side, TaoTao is litter-box trained, and she is cute and entertaining. Best of all, the girls think she's great. Rose is happy and agrees to continue going to school. (Bad parents?)

The next month we discover TaoTao has ear mites. Fortunately for us, there's a vet clinic on the first floor of our building. This is so much more convenient and will save us a bundle compared to ICVS, where we took TaoTao for her shots.

ICVS is an excellent Western vet clinic with English-speaking staff, but it takes about an hour to get there, it's complicated to find the actual building, and they charge Western prices. However, we will learn that the average Chinese vet and boarding facility are truly clueless when it comes to cats.

The vets and staff downstairs don't speak English, and our communication is done mainly through using a translation app and calling our friend, Jenny, to translate for us. For one little, six-pound kitten, it takes two vets and three vet techs to get her from behind the computer hard drive. The remaining vet has put on elbow length, leather gloves to protect himself from TaoTao's claws. He gets better at dodging the swipes to his face. The examination hasn't even begun. After three days of shots and ongoing treatment of ear wash and ear ointment, she's cured.

By December, it's time to have TaoTao spayed. On Christmas Day, Jim and I again take her to the clinic downstairs. Jenny has negotiated the procedure and price for us. Remember, the Chinese don't celebrate Christmas, so the girls are at school and the clinic is open. Most importantly, we can't stand another few weeks of her yowling at all hours of the day and night.

As adults, we've never had a cat before and at first, we think something must be terribly wrong with TaoTao. Jim keeps checking to see if she has been impaled by something. By searching online, we discover the obvious. We explain to the girls that TaoTao just wants a boyfriend. Ella states, "She's not going to attract anything acting like THAT."

We wonder what our Chinese neighbors are thinking. TaoTao is yowling at all hours, and it sounds like we're torturing something. We learn there's only one other pet cat in our building. So, cats as pets aren't prevalent and cat behavior isn't well known.

After weeks of the cat noises and the prospect of this continuing off and on for the rest of her life, we consider this operation a Christmas gift to ourselves and the world. At the end of the operation and a week of treatment with TaoTao's demeanor holding consistent with her initial visit, the vets have learned to say in perfect English, "Do not bring TaoTao back." I'm sure they can't possibly mean this.

Friends

We don't have or make a lot of friends in China, but the ones we do have are the best. We are also lucky enough to have several friends visit us.

Simon, Jenny and Daniel are our neighbors in our apartment building. We meet them on the elevator one day and exchange phone numbers. They invite us to a neighborhood restaurant one night, and the rest is history.

Pictured on the front row are Ella, Rose, and Makayla Thomas. Second row: me, Jenny and Daniel. Simon and Jim are in back.

Simon and Jenny are fluent in English. As a boy, Simon became very sick and had to miss a year of school. While bedridden, he studied English so diligently that he later was able to study in Ireland for his master's and Italy for his Ph.D.

Jenny has worked for American companies most of her life and speaks perfect English—she even knows our slang. One night at a restaurant, Jenny drinks Rose's water by mistake and says, "My bad!" I couldn't believe it. Jenny has never traveled outside of China, much less to an English-speaking country, so her ability to speak English so well amazes me.

Simon and Jenny are my go-to people when I don't understand how to do something or need to know where to find things. For example, we need winter clothing, and I have no idea where to look for children's clothes. It's a real challenge to shop when you've never heard of the stores or the brands. And American stores such as Gap are just too expensive.

Jenny takes us to the malls and stores where she shops for Daniel. These are VERY nice, high-end stores with excellent quality clothing. However, she learns how picky young American girls can be. Daniel, at their age, would wear whatever Jenny brought home. That stopped around age three with my two. Plus, even at nine and eleven years old, Ella and Rose won't wear the styles worn by Chinese children their age. They consider them "childish." For better or worse, my girls are more Justice and Abercrombie kids.

As a side bar, I find shopping in China frustrating. First off, clothes in China are no longer cheap unless you can find clothes made in China that stayed in China that you like. This doesn't happen very often. Plus, you won't find a helpful sales clerk. In traditional Chinese stores, the staff follows you around like white on rice. They're not helpful, but they're there.

With children's clothing, they don't put all the sizes out because of limited space. So, you have to ask for almost everything. Of course, their sizing system is different, different brands fit differently, and my kids keep growing, so it's usually impossible to know what size to ask for.

When shoe shopping, the Chinese don't measure your foot and again their sizing system is different. So, I just guess. Trying to ask which brands run wide and which run narrow never translates.

To sum it up, the Chinese are pretty much still clueless about customer service. It's like having an inept teenager wait on you, but they're adults.

Then, I find Uniqlo, which has clothing for the whole family. Of course, nothing except socks fit Jim, but what do you expect in Asia for a six-foot-tall slightly overweight man? I love the clothes. They're fun and the colors are great.

Now, back to Jenny and Simon—To demonstrate what a good friend and person Jenny is, she gives us Daniel's hand-me-downs to use for the winter. It's funny because we're both surprised to learn that hand-me-downs and donations of clothes to charity are common in both the U.S. and China. These clothes help so much and fill in the gaps as we shop. Jenny even lends me one of her winter coats until my sister arrives with mine.

Jenny and Simon are the reason I'm able to stay in China when Jim goes home for tax season. They tell me they'll help me in whatever way while Jim is gone, and they are true to their word. While Jim is back in North Carolina, Jenny and Simon have us to their place for dinner several nights, and when my cell phone is stolen, they guide me through the process of replacing it. When Simon goes abroad, usually to Switzerland, he brings us back chocolates. What better friends could you have?

To further demonstrate what a nice person Simon is, I have to tell you how Simon and Jenny met. Jenny and Simon are from the same province—Jiangsu. After individually visiting their families, they were taking a bus back to Beijing. The bus stopped suddenly, and Simon's suitcase fell from the overhead compartment, hit Jenny in the face, and broke her glasses. Simon says, "Of course, I had to get her address, so I could pay for her glasses. It was the luckiest day of my life." I'm not so sure Jenny, with broken glasses and a bruised face, was thinking this was so lucky, but isn't Simon just the nicest guy in the world?

OK, you're probably wondering about the other young girl in the picture, Makayla. This again was a bribe for Rose: "What would make you want to stay in China?" Answer, "Having one of my friends visit."

So, Makayla, who is one of Rose's classmates in Charlotte, is invited. As Makayla's mother says, "Makayla thinks she's part Chinese and would love to visit." So, Makayla is part of our family for three weeks. She is an extremely game and happy child, but just like all kids, she can sometimes be a handful. In the picture, we're in the subway getting ready to go to the train station for our tour of Jenny and Simon's home province.

Jenny and Simon are staples throughout our visit, but we meet another couple that pops in and out of our lives a few times. As mentioned earlier, I met Lloyd Riggins and his wife, Niurka Moredo, and their two children, Vianne and Oliver, at Wumart just after moving into our apartment in July. I like them immediately, and our families get together several times before they return home to Germany.

Lloyd is a principal dancer with the Hamburg Ballet, and Niurka is a retired dancer who now trains dancers with the Hamburg Ballet. They are in Beijing working with the National Ballet of China as they prepare to perform Hans Christian Anderson's The Little Mermaid.

Both Lloyd and Niurka are originally from the U.S. We bond over being foreigners in a different land, and we enjoy having someone who gets us. Aiding our friendship is that they are staying at a hotel just down the street from us.

When Lloyd returns without his family for a week to open The Little Mermaid, it's so good to see him.

The performance is amazing. Lloyd is pictured second from the right with no shirt and holding a bouquet. He dances the part of Hans Christian Andersen on the opening night. We don't see him afterward. He's waiting in his dressing room until he's paid for his performance. How interesting is that? So, knowing that he leaves for home early the next morning, we send him a note letting him know we were there and how much we enjoyed the performance. This is almost as exciting for me as the performance. The next day we get the nicest email from him.

This is the first performing-arts event we attend in China. To our amazement, the ballet venue is super convenient. It's on our bus line, Special Bus 30, near the west gate of The Temple of Heaven. It's a really nice, modern facility. This motivates us to seek out other arts events in Beijing.

Back to friends who are staples in our lives. Here we are at the stew restaurant with Cassie and Likan, now her husband. As you know by now, Cassie is the tutor for the girls and Jim during our first few months in Beijing, and she tutors Jim the last few months. Likan is working on his Ph.D. in Australia. So, this is the first time we meet him. We hope they will visit us in the States someday.

Sufang and Thomas are also staples for the year. Sufang is Chinese, but she and her husband immigrated to Oregon before Thomas was born. They have two sons, Fei, who attends college in the U.S., and Thomas, who's attending Beijing Yucai with the girls. Since I'm the only white person in the after-school pickup line, Sufang easily assesses me as American. She approaches me one day early on, and we become friends.

Thomas' father, who's a Chinese-trained doctor, moved back to China several years ago to advance his career. His mom was also a doctor in China but gave that up when the family moved to the States and has worked as a researcher at a university since. She and Thomas are now back in China for at least two years.

Then we have visitors. Ella's friend and classmate, Lorelei, arrives in early October for two days. She's touring China with her Chinese grandfather and mostly American-raised mother. We have a wonderful time with them.

Being with them breathes new life into us, as her grandfather does everything first class. When traveling with them, we have a nice minivan, driver, and guide. Her grandfather orders the best things on the menu and lives up to his reputation when we dine with them both nights.

After gaining permission from the school, Lorelei accompanies Ella to class one morning and then all of us girls travel to the Great Wall for the afternoon. Forget the views and the history, the highlight of this excursion is riding the mini cars from the Wall to the parking lot and seeing the bears in the "zoo" or inappropriate confinement area as I would call it.

After Lorelei's visit, my sister, Eve, visits the last two weeks in October. Here Eve and I are at Taoranting Park one morning after dropping off the girls at school. Eve stays in our apartment the first night, and then she hotel-hops to three different hotels (New Century Grand Hotel on Caishikou, Qianmen Jiangua Hotel on Yongan Lu, and The Crown Plaza on Wangfujing). Because of this, the girls get to spend a couple of nights in hotel luxury and have access to swimming pools, which they love.

We show Eve the sights we have enjoyed most. Rose takes Aunt Eve to the Temple of Heaven, I take her to the Summer Palace and Liulichang Culture Street near Meishi Lu for authentic Chinese souvenirs such as calligraphy brushes and paper, and as a family we enjoy a Peking duck dinner at Quanjude off Wangfujing. Here we watch the whole duck cooking process while we wait for our table. We all enjoy the Chinese acrobatics show at the Chaoyang Theatre and are amused at the Beijing Opera at the Liyuan Theatre in the Qianmen Jianguo Hotel, where Eve spends several nights.

I have to tell you about our Beijing Opera experience. We get the tickets from Lloyd and Niurka. Since they were long-term hotel guests at the hotel where a famous Opera theatre is housed, they were given tickets. They never used them and passed them on to us.

To our surprise and delight, these tickets are for the best seats in the house. We're seated at a dinner table in front where we are served tea and an assortment of snacks. Vignettes from several classic operas are performed. The symbolism and story of the operas being performed are projected on the walls on either side of the stage in English. It's very educational and well done.

However, Beijing Opera is definitely an acquired taste. I'm an American who prefers rock and roll, doesn't willingly opt for the symphony, and has been to only one opera because, again, I was given the tickets, and I could have split my sides laughing and rolled in the aisles at Beijing Opera. To the untrained, unindoctrinated ear, it sounds horrible. If I didn't know better, I would have thought it was a parody on opera in general. Thank God I have some restraint. If you have the opportunity, go but remember, I warned you.

Back to Eve ... she goes on a day tour with a tour group to the Great Wall, Ming Tombs and Forbidden City. Of course, several shopping excursions to acquire treasures at prices you will find nowhere else on one-of-a-kind merchandise are thrown in, as well as meeting someone related to an emperor who's now a famous artist. She returns well after dark, which has me a little panicked since we have no means of communication. As it turns out, the tour bus got stuck in Beijing traffic. Truly, another cultural experience no one should miss.

Commemorating Eve's departure, Simon, Jenny and Daniel take us all for a Chinese lunch complete with the fish head pointing at the honored guest. Jenny then takes us shopping at a nearby multi-story building with stalls selling everything from twine to electronics and clothing. We all buy some assortment of shoes, and Eve loads up on silk scarves for friends. All in all, I think Eve's visit gives her a good overview of Beijing and she has a good time.

Searching For The Perfect Massage

Ever since arriving in China, I have been searching for the ultimate massage that will cure my neck pain, be conveniently located, AND cost only $10 to $12 for an hour. This has led to many interesting experiences. My last experience almost ended my search.

Cassie and I find a VERY convenient place, which she initially thinks is fine. I want this to work so badly—the price is right, and it is SO convenient. When the woman in the high heels and low-cut dress asks me if I have a preference as to who gives me the massage, I say, "Anyone is fine." (Remember, I don't speak Chinese, and she doesn't speak English; Cassie is translating.) Then, she asks if I prefer a man or a woman—all reasonable questions, right? I say I could go either way.

All this time, I'm thinking the high-heeled woman is the receptionist. Now, when the door closes, and Cassie and I are on our separate tables in the same room, this woman starts the massage and wants to know if I think she's pretty. OK, I get the picture now. I tell Cassie I don't care what she looks like, just tell her to fix my neck. Afterward, Cassie asks what I think and then tells me my masseuse was a cashier last week. Great!

So, a couple of weeks later, Jenny shows me a new place that is also very convenient, and the price is right. She says it's very famous in Beijing. It's on a back street but has a very grand entrance like a nice hotel lobby. This is an actual spa where you can spend the day getting different treatments. There's even a large dining room serving a buffet meal during most of the day.

If nothing else, they're very good at up-selling. Jenny and I go there for foot massages, but Jenny ends up in a private room having a ninety-minute back massage with scraping and cupping. I stick with the fifty-minute neck and foot massage. (It pays not to understand what they're saying sometimes.) After my treatment, I join Jenny in time to get these pictures of her experience.

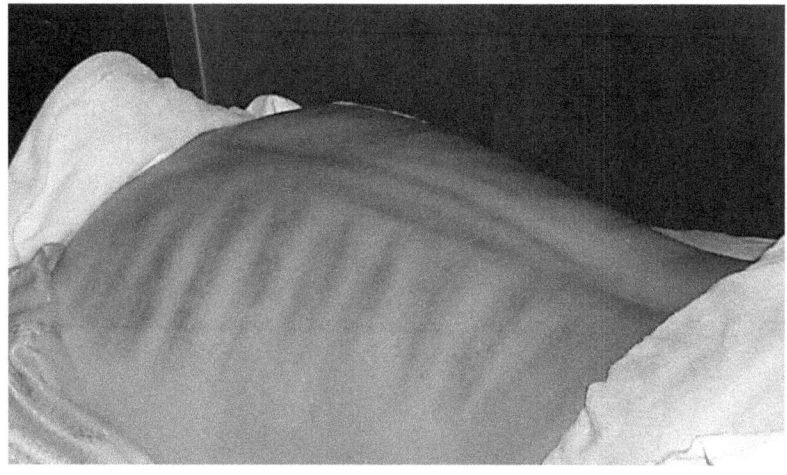

This is a picture of my friend, Jenny, getting a back massage that includes scraping. I will not be having this done.

Jenny's back is now being cupped

I go here several more times, but they take out the page in their services book with the foot massage for sixty yuan ($10). The least expensive treatment is now around $20. On my last two visits, the receptionist refuses to work with my gesturing and loudly states, "No one speaks English"—in English. I sense they don't want me or my American money, and around December I give up on my quest for the perfect massage in China. But, then there's Thailand.

Second Visa Trip: Trying to Get to Mongolia

Dinosaurs and wind turbines—so strange. This shot is taken along the road between town (Erlian, Inner Mongolia, China) and the airport.

Another sixty days has flown by and we are mandated to leave mainland China once again to satisfy our visa requirements. This time we're looking for a quick, cheap trip. I refuse to take the ten- to twelve-hour bus ride to Mongolia. At age twenty, I might have done this, but not now. So, Jim finds us flights on an airline that only books a week in advance. Wan, our landlord, happens by the apartment and helps with the phone call since it's all in Chinese.

When the plane lands and we all look out the window, Ella (remember she's nine) says, "Take me back to Beijing." She nails it. It's like the end of the Earth—nothing for miles. Flat ground with brown, dead grass because it's already winter here. It's literally freezing: zero degrees Celsius, at 4:00 in the afternoon.

The Foreigners Are in 709

We truly look like the stereotypical immigrants with our five layers of clothes and our scarves wrapped over our heads. It's October and beautiful in Beijing. What can I say? I told the girls to bring their winter coats. Did they listen? Of course not. I even took the coats out of their closets and laid them on their beds. Jim and I don't have winter coats yet—that's our excuse.

Anyway, turning back time for a moment, as we're sitting in the Beijing airport waiting to board the plane, we look up and there's a white person sitting right in front of us, facing us. We're the only white people anywhere to be seen. Is it happenstance we meet the only other foreigner in the terminal and he happens to be on our plane and just happens to be an American?

Michael is from LA and has been living in Beijing for three years. His Chinese is excellent, and he has done this trip several times. He goes to this Chinese border town to buy cigarettes in the duty-free and then sells them in Beijing for double, triple, whatever, the price. For most of the trip, we hang with him. He's helpful, but he adds to the strangeness.

Crossing the border into Mongolia is a bit tricky. Michael accompanies us in the cab from the airport to about a hundred yards of the border. Then, he orchestrates the car and the bus, which take us the remaining hundred yards. Yes, two different modes of transportation for one hundred yards. Money is being exchanged with everyone we encounter.

This whole experience reminds me of a scene from a Cold War Russian spy movie. There are old Russian military jeeps from that era, assorted other old military vehicles, and men in camouflage all around. It's very chaotic and scary. But it's comical, too, because the building we're trying to get to has a huge three-dimensional rainbow towering over it. Are they welcoming the LGBT segment? Is this truly the end of the rainbow? All sorts of thoughts run through my mind. I feel a little like we're playing a game of capture the flag and trying to make it to the rainbow.

It's hard to know what to do because no one speaks English, I don't think most people are even speaking Mandarin, and all signs are written in Cyrillic script. I'm literally afraid we might be shot and disposed of, never to be heard from again. Why would we be shot? I don't know. Maybe because we're just plain stupid.

To add to the dumb factor, we actually never make it to Mongolia. We make it into the building where China stamps our passports saying we have left China and into the duty-free area. Michael, of course, is busy trying to buy cigarettes and wants to buy our quota as well. For some reason, we get hustled out of there and are walking toward the Mongolian entrance building when a guard motions us back to the China entrance building. So, we go right back into China without ever entering Mongolia. It's so weird. I have no idea what is going on. More money is exchanged, and more forms are filled out.

Then all five of us get on a bus and we're dropped off in town. We stay at a hotel that looks nice—from the outside—where Michael has stayed before. The room is OK—just don't walk on the filthy carpet. (It's $60—expensive for what we get.)

The hotel looks as if it was built for a crowd and good times that never materialized. It has a whole lounge bar area with a disco that looks as if it has never been used but is worn with age and lack of attention. Miss Habersham would have been right at home here. It's very creepy.

We will experience this phenomenon several more times in our China travels where it looks as if venues were built for crowds that never came. Maybe we are just at these places in the off season, but it's very unsettling. In a way, these places prompt me to want to yell "Loser!" and run as fast as I can, but I'm afraid a monster might grab me and keep me there forever. This particular hotel and Erlian itself were expecting a growth spurt from oil that never materialized.

We eat dinner at a ridiculous Mongolian-themed restaurant, ordering too much food that costs too much ($80) for the five of us. Michael leaves us after dinner to meet a security guard from the duty-free to buy more cigarettes—strange. If drug trafficking weren't punishable by death in China, I would swear something besides cigs were being bought.

Sunday, the girls and I want to ride a camel, but when I point to the camel in a magazine and make hand gestures to the front desk clerk trying to ask where, she shakes her head "no," which we interpret as there aren't any. So, we go to the only other site in town—the dinosaur museum. Is this not fitting for this place?

This area of Inner Mongolia is known worldwide as a famous dig site for dinosaur fossils. The museum could be better, but there are all these life-sized dinosaur replicas all over a park surrounding the museum, which makes our visit fun.

One humorous incident happens at the museum. Some Chinese tourists ask to have their picture taken with me. However, they take pictures of just me. I can see the caption now in their photo albums—the almost extinct Hopeasourous. This takes me from being flattered to feeling like a relic. I can hear them telling their friends, "Look at the dinosaur we saw at the museum." Thanks a lot, guys. I REALLY feel old now.

Anyway, after a couple of hours, our cab that waited for us to complete the tour returns us to our hotel. We meet back up with Jim, who has taken a nap, and Michael, who has crossed the border yet again. I can only shake my head. The five of us take a cab back to the airport. We have an uneventful flight and are VERY glad to be back in Beijing. After Mongolia, Beijing seems less foreign to us and more like home. We never see Michael again.

Everyday Life in Beijing, October 14 – December 11

Here are some things that are just so Chinese to me. These are things we don't do or see in the U.S.

Traffic

The ever-present motor bike can carry generations of families. Motor bikes, bikes, and all assortment of motorized things with wheels are on the road—even electric wheel chairs. I almost got hit by one, so I know. The motor bike pictured below is so common. The little kids sit or stand in front. No one wears a helmet, but sometimes the kids wear elbow and knee pads. Explain that.

An American family livin' the life in China

How do you like these other contraptions? Packages are piled on top of carts for delivery, and bicycles are used for everything—in this case it's a terrarium. And how about the mobile bird cage? There are actually three exotic birds housed in the side bump-outs of this last "vehicle."

As you can imagine, as a city of twenty million, Beijing has some horrible traffic problems. To alleviate congestion, you have to enter a lottery and be selected to own a car. Once you get the car, drive time is contingent on whether your license number is odd or even. Then, the rules of the road are not like ours at home. Taking a left turn in front of oncoming traffic is common place. In short, the Chinese are horrible drivers. Sufang is our only friend who drives. She took a driving test in the U.S. five times before passing. Does this not prove my point?

The Getup

The purpose of taking this picture is to get the woman with the bike who was my elevator mate—yes, bike and all. Note the fashionable visor and the opera-length gloves from finger to shoulder. Quite the look. The purpose is to keep the sun off and the skin a light tone. Believe it or not, you see this quite a bit. I've also seen a few Asians in the U.S. with the visor.

Brooms

There are no gas or electric blowers here. The public sanitation people and everyone else use these big old-fashioned brooms. It seems archaic at first, but I like not hearing the constant hum of blowers.

Dusters

Check out the man dusting the roof of his car. Beijing is a dusty, polluted city, and most Chinese are very proud of their cars, so they actually dust the exteriors. The dusters are kept in the trunk ready at a moment's notice for a quick swipe.

Crowds

If you don't have a car, the subway is a great option, but it can be crowded. The following picture shows Rose and Ella in rush hour. Several times during our year's stay, I have to get off one train and try the next because it's too claustrophobic. However, it's not always this crowded. Many times, we even get seats.

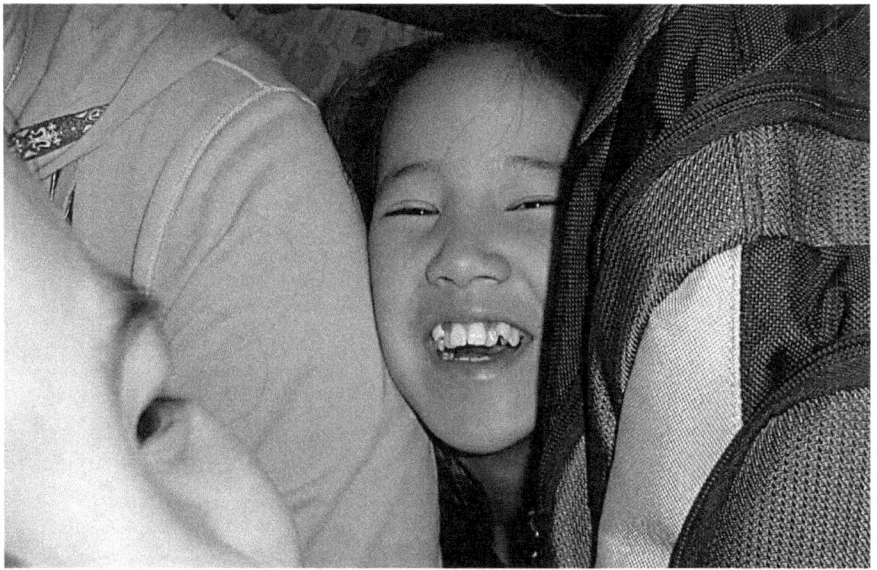

A big cultural difference we find in China is that the Chinese don't line up for many things. I'm used to first-come, first-served, but I quickly learn this doesn't happen in China. In fact, even when I'm the first in line for the subway, airplane, elevator—it doesn't matter what—and determined to be first, I'm still middle of the pack or last when time comes to board or exit. The Chinese aren't outright rude; they just push ahead and subtly use their elbows.

I don't have these skills because I get mad and aggressively use my elbows.

Long before this trip, I noticed and marveled at how Ella always ends up in front of lines. In preschool and at toddler parties, Ella always found her way to the front of any line or group, usually holding hands with the adult leader. Now I know it's just part of her DNA. In China, she always makes her way through the crowds. So, I learn to just follow Ella.

Pictures

This just cracks me up. There is a sign that says not to touch the statuary, but does this make a difference? ... No! The Chinese do all sorts of things for a good picture, including trampling flowers, climbing on monuments, and posing incessantly.

Ready for Winter

You know it's going to be getting cold when ... the bike gloves and blankets are attached to the motor bikes ...

...Fifi dons her new winter coat, (Dog clothing is rampant. A woman I tutor has a dog named Happy. Happy has more shoes than I do. She even has her own shoe rack by the front door.)

...and the quilted door covers are attached to entrances.

How I See Life In China

This picture pretty much sums up our everyday life: It's somewhat like home but different. At home, we have Walmart, here we have Walmart and Wumart—the Chinese equivalent of Walmart. Wumart's almost like Walmart but not quite. It smells different, the layout is different with two stories, a lot of the food is different, they don't sell some things I want, and mostly everything's written in Chinese.

In a new place, no matter where you are, another U.S. city for that matter, the differences throw you off. It's a little uncomfortable. Everything has a bit of a learning curve. Unlike in your own familiar surroundings, where you're used to how things work, you have your routines and you don't think about everyday stuff constantly, life can be more of a challenge in any new place.

To be truthful, life in Beijing is a little more different because at home we mainly go to Target, which sadly hasn't hit China yet. If you're a Target shopper, you know what I mean. Now that I think about it, how I see China compared to the U.S. is a little like comparing Target to Walmart. Just bear with me. Walmart and Target have similar merchandise, but Target is cleaner and trendier, and the items are better displayed. It's the same with the U.S. and China. The two countries have a lot of the same things, but things in general are cleaner, trendier, and better displayed in the U.S.

China reminds me of what the U.S. probably was like in the 1950s and early '60s. The middle and upper middle class are growing by leaps and bounds. There are lots of people doing VERY well here. Smoking is rampant; dresses are short, and social drinking is in vogue, but drugs (prescription or illegal) are not used by the masses. There are tons of low-rise buildings giving way to skyscrapers. There's a lot of modernization, and the young are focused on the future, not the old customs of China.

I get a taste of the more affluent Chinese lifestyle when I do several promotional shows for an English language school in a park that wealthier families flock to.

Here are Ella and Rose on stage between shows of our English language promotional. Xi Yang, a cartoon character, is to the left.

It costs thirty-three cents to go to Taoranting Park, the park near our apartment. Rabbit Park, where this event takes place, costs fifteen dollars per person. I'm the only one here with a cheap point-and-shoot camera. Everyone else has a multiple lense, telescopic camera and is feverishly snapping shots of their only child wearing outfits with high-end labels.

Digressing a bit and being a little catty: The twenty-two-year-old woman who is the host of our English show, Grace, wears a sweater with tights and high-heeled boots—remind anyone of the sixties? The sweater is so short that it barely covers her rear. I tell Rose and Ella I want to do an English lesson on clothing titled "Where are Grace's pants?"

Anyway, getting back on track, China is very money conscious. Brand names are everywhere and heavily sought after. Anyone who has money wears only clothes from the best stores, and they like the labels showing.

The businessman I tutor in English grills me one day on the best purse brand. His wife says Louis Vuitton is not the best. I'm the wrong woman to be asking. I assure him that Louis Vuitton is a very good brand. He also compliments my teeth and says he's heard Americans are very particular about their teeth.

Here's a big tip. Just as "plastics" was the word in the 1960s, I believe "orthodontia" is the word in China for the 2020s. The Chinese in general have horrible teeth, and just think of how many mouths there are.

Another aspect of Chinese life that is a throwback to the American 1950s is how safe it is. It's against the law to own a gun in China, and there are no visible signs of illegal drugs unless you actively seek them out. As a woman, I don't worry about walking alone at night or being on the subway or in a cab. Rose and Ella can go into the neighborhood hutong to get snacks, dinner, whatever, and the only thing we warn them about is to watch for traffic.

Our Daily Life

On a typical weekday, we are up around six a.m. The girls and I are at the bus stop to catch Special Bus 30 at 6:50. This city bus only runs weekdays during rush hour and makes a circle. Unfortunately, we must get off, wait and then reboard the bus two stops before the school. Therefore, it saves time to get off a few blocks from the school and walk. The stop we choose is in front of a restaurant that sells baozi and youtiao (dumplings and fried bread). We usually buy one or the other and eat it on the way, or we go around the corner to a food stall to make our purchase of shao bing with a fried egg. Everything is made to order. It's so good, fresh, and unhealthy.

Jim is teaching a math class at a public high school and takes the subway. I drop the kids, take the bus to the subway, and then take another bus to help a woman with her English. On two afternoons, I also help a man with his English. We have met some nice people this way, and it's also forced us to explore other parts of the city.

In the afternoons, either Jim or I walk to the school—about thirty minutes—to meet the girls. There are about ten to fifteen little stores and stands that sell school supplies and snacks in the one block between the school and the bus stop. Rose and Ella always need a snack, and for some reason Ella always needs more school supplies. However, she buys them with her own money, so I don't complain. I later learn that Ella is the class "dealer." Since her classmates all board at the school, Ella is buying their supplies and is getting paid in trinkets. Good little American entrepreneur.

At 4 p.m., Special Bus 30 starts again, and we catch it for the trip home. It drops us just across the street from our apartment. By 5, we're all home. The tutor comes at 5:30 for two hours on Wednesdays and Fridays, and tonight the maintenance man is here to fix the slow draining sink in the kitchen and some things in the bathroom.

I cook dinner about two or three nights a week. It's always some type of pasta with vegetables, and we have fruit. There is a market in the hutong that sells everything. I can buy two pounds of homemade pasta for two yuan (thirty-three cents) and any kind of fruit or vegetable. They also sell meat, but I don't buy meat here in China because I'm not sure what I'm buying. For those of you who know Jim, you'll appreciate that he has found a local grocery two blocks away for his Diet Coke fix.

On other nights, we get take-out from one of the restaurants nearby or eat out. For breakfast, we buy Muesli cereal online, from WuMart, Walmart or the convenience store by the Holiday Inn Temple of Heaven. Or, we buy the street food I mentioned.

Our Neighborhood

Following are pictures of my walk home from the Taoranting subway stop one afternoon. These are the typical things I see day in and day out.

Here's the neighbor lady walking her pooches with their coats on. There are short little dogs everywhere in Beijing. The most common are chocolate poodles. The reason for all the little dogs is yet another news flash for me. Along with China's one-child policy, Beijing has a one-dog policy. Who knew?

The stipulations of the policy are as follows: All dogs must be registered; one dog per family, no ferocious breeds, and every dog must be fourteen inches or less in height. It began in 2006 to curb the spread of rabies. In 2005, 69,000 Beijing citizens sought treatment for rabies—this is just in Beijing—and only three percent of dogs were vaccinated against it. I don't know why height figures in, but that's the rule. Of course, there are ways around the rules. Since she has two dogs, one may be registered in another province or maybe it's her neighbor's dog. If you have multiple dogs, you just don't talk to your neighbors about them. If people ask, you're vague.

This is the fruit and vegetable stand we pass all the time. We buy from here sometimes, but we usually buy from the bigger market just up the street. However, I like this stand. It's always so fresh and pretty. I consider it my still life.

This stall is next to the fruit stand. We buy our toilet paper here and occasionally ice cream. We prefer the toilet paper on the roll, which is priced a bit higher but the one without the roll tends to fall into the toilet, making it ultimately the more expensive choice.

We sometimes buy our tomatoes and other veggies from these carts. How smart is this? The cart is attached to the bicycle for easy relocation.

All means of transportation go through this hutong, except for buses. Note the pizza delivery on the bike. McDonald's even has bike delivery.

This is the entrance to our apartment complex. There is a guard in the glass area to the right 24/7.

I have now turned into our apartment complex, passed the guard and will head up the steps. The recycling bin is front and center. I love this recycling concept where the recycling cart is attached to a bike. Again, how great is this? When the cart's full, it's just cycled over to the recycle center around the corner.

Once entering the building, I take a right down a short, poorly lit hallway and a left, which puts me here by the stairwell and elevators. It's not very grand, but it's home. The Chinese don't take very good care of their lobby areas in general.

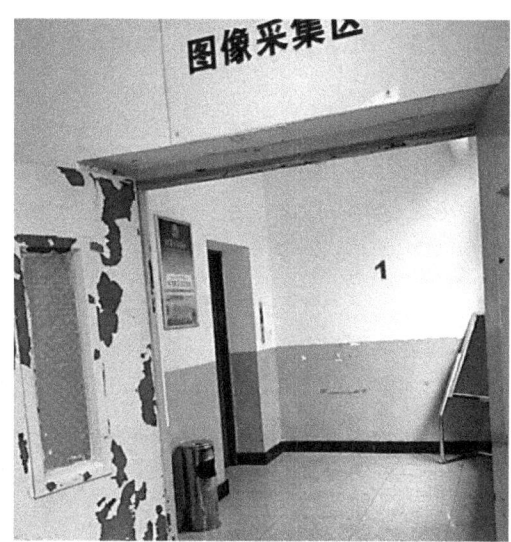

Now, I'm leaving the neighborhood and showing you our other regular haunts. These are a bit more modern.

Rose and Ella are at the basement food court at Capital Mall at Xizhimen. This is my favorite mall. It's where subway Lines Four, Thirteen, and Two meet. So, it's easy to get to and it has the best Uniqlo store.

The noodle dish Rose and Ella are eating is great. It's homemade noodles with a peanut sauce over greens served cold. I sometimes get this as take-out for dinner.

Yes, Communist China's official stand on religion is atheism, but Christmas decorations do appear in some parts of town. This Rudolph is being erected the week before Thanksgiving in the Sanlitun area of Beijing. This area is known for its bar scene. It's also where I'm told you can buy lots of things illegally including drugs. It's a very trendy and Western area. The embassies are near here.

If I want to see another Westerner living in Beijing, I come here. However, I find most of these people aren't very friendly. They don't make eye contact and almost never say hello in passing. I find this depressing. I make friends with no expats the whole year and find this odd.

I originally find this area through my tutoring student who lives in an upscale apartment beside this mall. She introduces me to the Hello Kitty Restaurant on the third floor of the mall that is upbeat with all its Hello Kitty decorations and Hello Kitty-shaped food. It has a diner feel with pink booths, milk shakes and other diner-type food, and it's reasonably priced. We eat at Hello Kitty several times as a special treat and as a mood pick-me-up.

My favorite store, Uniqlo, has a huge location in Sanlitun. It's a Japanese chain, and I love it. It's a trendy Lands' End if that's not an oxymoron. Uniqlo sells men's, women's, and children's clothing—everything from underwear to parkas. Every week they reduce something wonderful and then it goes back to the regular price the following week. I go every week to see what's on sale. Yes, this is my addiction.

Heat

We have our very first snow on Sunday, November 4. Beijing gets skiffs of snow—just inches, not feet. Since then, the weather has been nice with highs in the 40s to 50s. But, due to the early snow, China turns on the heat a little bit earlier this year.

What? This is news to me. How can you not just turn on your own heating system and have a thermostat to control it? Jim is familiar with living in rent-controlled buildings in New York City where building management regulates the heat supply, but in this situation, the Chinese government is in control.

From what I have since read, the government supplies "central heating" for Northern China officially from November 15 to March 15, but because China is trying to be more progressive, this can vary. The timing is now based on whether the daily average outdoor temperature is less than or equal to 5 degrees Celsius (41 degrees Fahrenheit).

Our friend Jenny has gone home to Jiangsu Province to take care of her sick mother. Her hometown is just above Shanghai, and there is no heat there. In the days of Mao, no city south of the Yellow River was to have heat—no fire places, no nothing but warm clothes and heavy blankets. And so, it is today. Winter clothes for kids are padded for warmth, and they use hot water bottles and heavy quilts to warm their beds. It baffles me why there are no household or commercial heating systems. From what I have read, it's because of Chinese energy policies and cost.

I subsequently meet a man from Russia who moved from Shanghai to Beijing because he couldn't bear the cold all day in his office building. I asked if Russia has similar heat policies. He emphatically said, "Absolutely not."

Thanksgiving In China

This year we're the pilgrims celebrating with the natives—I like this twenty-first-century twist on the traditional American holiday story. We have made Thanksgiving dinner reservations at Lily's American Diner at 6 p.m. to share this very American holiday with our friends.
We chose this restaurant because it's supposed to be somewhat close by, it serves American food, it's reasonably priced, and they've advertised a traditional Thanksgiving dinner menu. We've never been here, but hope it's good because we've invited Jenny, Simon, and Daniel and Sufang, Thomas and Thomas' dad to dine with us.

Like us, Thomas is in his first year of living in China. He and our girls bond over "weird" Chinese school customs. The tradition of the adults' and kids' tables somehow sneaks in. Thomas, Rose, and Ella are sitting behind us at a counter that seats three very nicely. There is constant conversation and laughter coming from the three of them the whole evening. The fact they are seated separate from us turns out to be very prophetic as the night wears on.

The evening begins with stress. Daniel is late getting home. So, at 6 p.m., the six of us are just starting to try to catch a cab—with absolutely no luck, and it's REALLY cold. So, our family takes a black cab. To make a long story short, it takes us an hour to get to Lily's, and we're the first of our party to arrive. The others arrive within twenty minutes of us. It doesn't help that the restaurant sign is about the size of a laptop.

The place is tiny but nice. Everyone eating here is American and in a very festive holiday mood. The food is the traditional turkey, dressing, potatoes and gravy, pumpkin pie meal, which is exactly what we want. Everything looks and tastes great. We talk, we laugh, and we even run into another family whose son goes to Beijing Yucai.

Jim and I are the hosts, so we treat everyone. It's a wonderful, feel-good holiday time for all of us. Jim and I congratulate ourselves on what a nice evening we've arranged and shared as we sit with the girls in the warm, cozy cab on our way home.

At 1 a.m., the lights go on. As we are cleaning up the vomit from the floor in the girls' room and listening to foul sounds coming from the bathroom, we wonder who else is sick. Apparently, the lights went on at Thomas' house at the exact same time. After making the calls the next morning to inquire about everyone's health, we determine that the three at the children's table seem to be the only casualties. Thank God!

Lesson learned—when a country doesn't routinely serve a food, don't order it. Next time we're in China for Thanksgiving, we'll have Peking duck.

Sufang calls the restaurant. In true Chinese style, she tells the restaurant manager, "Your restaurant poisoned our children." The restaurant manager advises her that "If the children need emergency services, you need to be calling the hospital." This exchange of exaggerated facts and no acceptance of guilt are so common in China. It makes me laugh. Happy holidays, y'all.

Teaching

Once Rose and Ella are settled into the routine of school, Jim and I start our illustrious careers with Jim posting our thrown-together resumes online. We decide to do this for some extra cash and to get us out of the house.
Within two hours, we are traveling to Tianjin (an hour from Beijing) on a "teaching" assignment. We later figure out that we are the token white English speakers in a sales scheme to sign up unsuspecting students at a new after-school English franchise. But the company pays for our whole family's travel expenses, we get to see Tianjin, and we learn some things.

After our initial weekend gig in Tianjin, I do the English school promo during the week of the Moon Festival at Rabbit Park for Easy English that I mentioned earlier.

Again, I am the token white English-speaking person luring Chinese children into yet another after-school activity. However, I find this emceeing experience to be a real kick. I've never before co-emceed an event on a stage in a park or anywhere else for that matter. To be totally truthful, I have a fear of public speaking. But the weather is beautiful, and I have an audience twice a day that for the most part doesn't know what I'm saying and listens intently. It's very liberating.

Aside from bestowing unplanned self-confidence, the job has two other perks. Rose and Ella, who accompany me twice, get into the park for free. With only one point of entry and exit, the girls can safely explore the park while I'm doing my thing. The other perk is that the head guy buys me lunch most days and sometimes drops me at the subway instead of my having to find a taxi.

I do become a tad bitter, though, toward this company. I learn the Chinese take a two-hour break, similar to the Spanish siesta, for which there's no pay. So, working 10 to 4 means I'm really only working four hours. Plus, everyone but me is getting paid double because it's a holiday, and on top of that, I learn I'm underpaid as a fluent English speaker at 120 yuan/hour ($20). From then on, I don't take a job for less than 150 yuan ($25) per hour. Adding insult to injury, I'm never compensated for the time I spent at the school and at home planning the English portion of "the show."

Looking back over all my teaching assignments, what I find is that in general, the people in charge of these English "schools" are unorganized and they don't pay for anything but teaching hours. In this case, I complain to the company, never receive any additional compensation, and am never again available when they call, but I learn a lot about working in China.

For my next work assignment, I'm the teacher in an English-speaking video series. To my surprise, they ask me to sign a release. I'm still frightened that someday I may live to regret this. Each video opens with *Yankee Doodle*, which I sing and march to. I'm horrible, but I can't think of anything else to do and just standing there looking stupid doesn't seem right either. In hindsight, maybe I should have just stood there. Anyway, again, I'm part of something I've never been asked to do before—and probably never will be again. Wistfully though, I think maybe somewhere some class is watching and learning English from me or ... having a really good laugh.

I also record some English science tapes one afternoon, but my main source of work comes from tutoring and teaching a class. For one company, Gooden English, I tutor assorted adults. My stints with my tutoring clients last for varied lengths of time. Gooden provides no curriculum, and my teaching material is limited to the books they have collected from past students. The businessman I tutor provides his own book on business terminology, which is quite good with vocabulary, dialogues, and a practice tape. I'm with him the longest at about three months.

My classroom work consists of teaching a group of seven-year-olds on Sunday mornings from 10 a.m. to noon at Vanthink School. I enjoy all of my teaching jobs, but my best job in every way is this little Sunday class. The school provides me with a great series of books to teach from, they only praise my work, and I love the kids.

This is my Sunday class at Vanthink School

At this school, I am a rock star, and I love it. With a cameraman present, I do some two-hour "English Corners" which are promotionals to recruit new students. My permission is asked to use my picture for marketing efforts. I get to be creative with my classes, and we have a blast—most days. The job lasts from the fall until our scheduled departure in June. Did I mention that they treat me like a rock star?

After class, I go to lunch with the Sandies. "Big Sandy", the mom, approaches me early on and asks if I will tutor Little Sandy after class. In place of payment, I ask that she feed me lunch.

This develops into a nice friendship. I learn a lot about Chinese food, and Big Sandy shows me some shopping spots. Both the mom and daughter speak very good English. Big Sandy likes to watch American movies and says this is how she's learned English so well. She wants Little Sandy to visit the U.S. Maybe one day soon.

Thomas is my best student. We get each other. In the beginning, he acted up in class and then, one day things just clicked: He started doing everything I asked him, he wanted to do his work, and do it right. Having this type of connection with a student is amazing.

Then, there's Andersen, Elaina, Peter, and Angel. Andersen is the biggest cut-up, and Elaina is the quietest. Peter knows the least English, but he has a good time. Angel is the chattiest, mainly in Chinese but her English is excellent, and she's helps the others. Aren't they the cutest kids ever? I miss them.

Overall, I find fulfillment in teaching. With tutoring, I go to the student—home, office or coffee shop. This takes me to places I never would have discovered on my own. For the most part, I like figuring out the public transportation route—the subway and/or buses—and discovering new places and people.

The only time I'm really frightened is when I'm sent to meet the businessman at his office. I'd been there once before by taxi. This time, they send me by subway and then bus on my own dime. I can tell the bus isn't taking me anywhere near my destination, so I get off and luckily, easily catch a cab.

With my new iPhone 4S, I show the cab driver the text from my employer with the address written in Chinese. Remember, my Chinese is minimal, and the driver speaks no English. As he drives me around, the area doesn't look familiar—at all. I get my employer and the driver on the phone. The driver takes me in another direction, stops, and I get out to see whether I recognize anything.

I think leaving my phone with the driver is best because he surely wouldn't leave me when he has my phone—right? Once I get out, I think … Yes, he just might take off with my cell phone, idiot. Remember the taxi driver who swiped our computer? Let's just say this experience teaches me to never, ever be separated from my phone again. I realize how valuable that phone is to my very existence.

So, I'm outside the taxi in the southwestern outskirts of Beijing—no English speakers are within miles. Scary thoughts are racing through my head. It feels like a version of the American Wild West before trouble comes to town. Run-down shacks dominate the scenery. The sun is beating down. No one is in sight. A slight breeze blows tumble weed (no joke) across the dusty street. There are only a couple of stray dogs looking for cover (probably rabid). I fear I may get left and never find my way home. I run the five steps back to the car and anxiously ask for my iPhone.

I then get my student, the businessman, on the phone with the driver, and in ten minutes, I'm at my destination. The businessman gives me the correct subway stop and bus number to ride next time and walks me to the bus stop when our session is over. I think he thinks I might be directionally impaired because he continues to walk me to the bus stop until another transportation option occurs two months later. When subway Line Ten is completed and the Xiju stop is added, his office is a straight shot and an easy two-block walk. No buses or taxis needed.

Overall, I really enjoy my English jobs. The jobs put me in places—literally and figuratively—I would never have imagined. I earn some spending money, learn a lot, keep my sanity, and I hope, teach my students a little English. I also think I'm a good ambassador for America—a holdover expectation from my exchange-student days.

Back in the States, when I tell friends how much I loved my teaching experiences, they ask if I'd like to teach in the U.S. I say, "Hell no." What made it fun was the randomness and feeling like a rock star. I don't think that's going to happen here at home.

Third Visa Trip: Bangkok, Thailand— A Great Place

We've chosen Thailand as our next trip necessitated by our visa. You can do things in Thailand legally that I've never seen anywhere else. Where can you hold and feed a seven-month-old leopard you just happen upon on the street? Where can you pet and walk with tigers and Buddhist monks? Thailand, of course.

Bangkok and our one-day excursion that includes the floating market, a long boat ride through the jungle, the Bridge over the River Kwai, and the Tiger Temple, are truly fantastic. Thailand's the kind of place I dream about—around every corner is an unexpected, fun surprise. The streets are filled with vendors selling fresh fruit, freshly made food, crafts, and clothes, and they're nice. Oh, and it's warm—ninety-degree highs in December.

Our hotel—Centre Point Silom—is the greatest ($80/night including two buffet breakfasts. Additional breakfasts for children are $5.50 each). We have a one-bedroom, one-bath efficiency, which is spacious, clean, well appointed, luxurious, and everything else nice. The hotel pool is big and sparkling with stacks of freshly laundered guest towels and food service available. The buffet breakfast is the best we encounter in all our travels with made-to-order omelets, French toast, pancakes, beautiful fresh fruit (Ella tries Jack fruit for the first time and loves it), cereal, fruit juices, and multiple Thai and Western entrées.

In addition, the location can't be beat. It's right behind the Shangri-La and the Mandarin Oriental hotels. We are one block from the river pier and a block from the Sky Train—(Bangkok's mass transit). The hotel is connected to Richardson's Department store, which has a great Western grocery store (Tops Market) in the basement and a food court. There's a Mister Doughnut attached, too. For some reason, we really miss doughnuts and are uncharacteristically elated whenever we see a real one.

There's a huge Thai market across from the hotel entrance selling fresh flowers and all manner of food and drink. Stores with all sorts of exotic trinkets line the street. We also find several excellent, inexpensive restaurants around the corner.

Did I mention that Thailand is a great bargain? Food, accommodations, clothing, silk, transportation, and sightseeing are all unbelievably reasonable. The Thai people also have an imagination and make things fun and colorful. The hotels, restaurants, and sights are clean and have a good vibe. Our five days are filled with sightseeing—the Grand Palace and Wat Phrakeaw (Wat means temple) with the emerald Buddha and Wat Pho with the reclining Buddha—eating well, shopping, and soaking in the sunshine by the pool.

Fourth Visa Trip: Did I Tell You We Love Thailand...

This fruit stand is the beginning of the
Thai Market by our hotel

It's the end of January now, and yes, we're back in Thailand. We're again staying at the Centre Point Silom, which you know we love. This time we even have a washer/dryer in our room—love it. The fridge and mini kitchen come in even handier for our two-week stay in Bangkok. I never cook because the food here is so good and cheap, but we do have leftovers to store and reheat.

The reason we are back in Thailand is twofold. First, we need to get our Chinese visas renewed. Our current visas expire at the end of February, and to renew them we must leave mainland China and send our passports back to the

U.S., to a Chinese consulate. We are using the same company we originally used.

We're trying for a six-month visa with ninety-day stays. Going through the San Francisco Consulate office, we learn that we can get a six-month visa, but we'll have to leave China every thirty days. Leaving every sixty days has been manageable but leaving every thirty days seems a bit overwhelming. Our passports are now going to the D.C. Consulate to try for the ninety-day stay.

Once we get back our passports with visas, we can travel again. Not having a passport in hand is a big deal. As foreigners, we can't check into a hotel or board a plane or train without valid passports. Basically, we're stuck in Bangkok in The Centre Point Silom Hotel until we have passports again.

This is the best place in the world, except for home, that I could possibly think of being stuck. However, all this still makes me a little claustrophobic and very stressed when dealing with what will become "the nitwits" at the visa company.

The other reason we're in Thailand is that it's winter break in China. For Chinese New Year, the girls get a four-week vacation from school. It's literally freezing in Beijing—the coldest winter on record in thirty years. But in Thailand, it's in the high 80s and low 90s. Plus, Thailand is a wonderful bargain. What would you do?

Jim returned to the U.S. for three months for tax season. He left December 28, 2012. We miss him, but as I like to tell it—someone has to make money to support our travels and my new-found addiction to all things silk. So, it's me and the girls. However, today we're REALLY missing Jim. How do single parents do it?

We can eat, tour, shop and hang out by the pool only so long. Poor us! After three days of a *Hannah Montana*—how many shows can we watch a day?—marathon, I have instituted a thirty-minute-per-day TV and computer limit and thirty-minute-plus English reading time for the girls. Let's see how long I can stand enforcing this without backup.

The girls are asking if they can put the duvet cover on the floor. No!..... Several hours later—I've been on the computer this whole time—I look up. The bed has been moved to another corner of the room, I don't see the duvet cover, and the girls are running water in the bathroom. Ella comes out to ask what I'm doing, and I think I need to ask her the same question. "Stuff" is her answer. I gotta go.

We have a great day at Jim Thompson's house. This picture is taken at the house and shows a man demonstrating how silk threads are made from silkworm cocoons. Here he's adding coal to the fire.

We watch him boil the cocoons in the pot and use the forked stick to bring up silk strands to the roller where they are combined into one thread. It takes about ten strands to make one silk thread. The silk is then collected in a basket.

The sad thing is that the worms are killed during the process. Because of this, Buddhist monks, who heavily populate Thailand, disapprove of silk making. In the early 1950s, this and other factors converged to diminish the demand for silk, including limited usage because of fading and the advent of machines making other fabrics faster and cheaper.

Enter an American, Jim Thompson, who revived the industry with his sense of design and color and his business savvy. I love this man. He's truly an international man of mystery. Here's a brief history to stimulate your curiosity.

Jim Thompson was born in 1906 and well educated, including Princeton. He's also well-traveled in North Africa and Asia including Thailand during his stint with the OSS (the predecessor of the CIA) during World War II. He saw the potential of Thailand as a travel destination as well as a silk producer for the sophisticated and moneyed.

He commissioned several lengths of silk in a range of colors woven to his design specifications, which he showed to the editor of *Vogue* magazine. The editor soon published an edition of the magazine featuring Valentino, the dress designer, wearing a Thai silk garment. With this endorsement, other influential people became acquainted with Thompson's Thai silk, and it started being used on Broadway and in other high-profile places. Thompson initiated strict standards, introduced colorfast dyes, and quickened the weaving process. So began a thriving industry that continues today.

On the personal side, Thompson was the ultimate entertainer and lived a very large life in Thailand. To send him a letter, you needed only his name and Bangkok on the envelope. Until one day, in 1967, he went out for a walk and never was seen or heard from again. No trace of him has been found. I'm leaving it here because you should really read his complete story. He's just a fascinating man. Someone should make a mega movie about this man.

The girls and I can attest to the fact that his Thai Silk Company is still thriving. I drag Rose and Ella to as many of his stores in Bangkok as I can, including spending one glorious afternoon at his outlet. The outlet even has a café on the top floor that is amazingly good—best burger in a long time, but pricey. Everything about the stores (even the outlet) and merchandise is still top notch. Every detail is attended to. How this level of quality has been maintained over so many years would make for an incredible business study.

If you decide to check out the outlet, getting there by the sky train is fairly easy. It's a five to ten-minute walk from the train exit and well worth it. There are a few local shops along the way that are interesting, too.

To visit the Muslim silk cottages, walk along the klong (canal) in front of Thompson's home and cross the pedestrian bridge. There's an outdoor restaurant at the bridge if you're hungry or thirsty. Once you cross the bridge, if you really search, you will find a few cottages dyeing, weaving, and selling silk. It's one of our best experiences in Bangkok, but I love hole-in-the-wall places. Here are Ella and Rose in the attic of a cottage silk shop, TT Piligan Thaisilk International.

The Foreigners Are in 709

The family who owns it made silk for Jim Thompson. There's a picture on the entry wall of the father (now seventy-three years old) in his teens with Jim Thompson.

We enjoy the hotel pool pretty much every day. Today, the girls are especially happy to see the elephant fountains have been turned on. This just adds a little more fun.

We are usually lucky and get three pool chairs in the upper right corner where there's shade. Today, we aren't so lucky. Can I just say it's unbelievable what some adults—most well over sixty—will do for what I have learned are prime spots?

These "adults" have come out early and put their belongings on the chairs to "save" them. Two chairs open up for which my girls are next in line, but this young Thai female with a considerably older Western gentleman race around the pool—literally—and throw their stuff on them. I spend too much of the afternoon seething and thinking about what I would like to tell the old man who is with someone a quarter of his age: "No, no, you take the chairs, you're much older than I, and your daughter probably hasn't ever been to a pool before."

This book is meant for family reading, but you adults can read between the lines. This is one thing I don't like about Thailand. Why don't these people just stay in their rooms and stop taking my lounge chairs?

We have some huge technical difficulties. This is how it goes down. We are in Bangkok at the hotel, Ella is on the computer—which we lugged, cords and all, so we could Skype with Jim—and all goes black. I'm frantic wondering how we will communicate with Jim. Rose solves our Skype problem by installing the Skype app on my iPhone. If I'd known about this app, I never would have brought the laptop. I'm torn between hugging and screaming at Rose. And so, are the days of our lives....

We stay in Bangkok a few more days than expected. This is because our Chinese visas take longer than expected— "the nitwits" at the visa company truly messed up with no apology. We are disappointed to get six-month, thirty-day visits and swear never to use that visa company again.

We visit the Dusit zoo, which is really fun. We sit in the front row at the elephant show. There is nothing between us and the elephants, who are just a few feet away. However, my worry isn't about the well-trained elephants per se. I'm more worried about a tiny animal. The school girl next to me has shown me a small pet rodent she has in her bookbag.

In the back of my mind, I'm remembering some story where elephants are deathly afraid of mice and go on a rampage. Is this an old wives' tale? Should we move a few rows back? Is the rodent properly secured? Should I say something? This whole thing is so odd. Why would anyone have a rodent in her backpack? Why would you bring it to a zoo? I sit and watch the show with one eye on the backpack ready to scoop up my children and run at a moment's notice.

The seal show is a bigger hit with the girls even though a pigeon poops on Rose's head. The silver lining is that a bird pooping on your head is a symbol of good luck in Asian cultures. How lucky. We tour the rest of the zoo, which is amazing, and get double-scoop ice cream cones for around 50 cents. Another great day in paradise.

Another day we visit Wat Arun, which is a temple on the west side of the river. You can climb all over it and take amazing photos. The colors, patterns, and materials are just mind-boggling beautiful. Plus, the coffee and tea stand has delicious beverages. OK, maybe I'm just tired and thirsty, but my tea drink tastes great.

Standing on the second level
looking up at Wat Arun

Here's a close-up of the incredible
tile decorating Wat Arun

With passports in hand, we fly north to Chiang Mai on February 8 for seven days. Chiang Mai is even more of a bargain than Bangkok. I book a $30/night hotel room including breakfast on the Northeast corner of the Old Town—FX Royal Panerai. I wouldn't necessarily recommend it, but it turns out to be clean and in a good location. Remember, I'm booking all this on a teeny, tiny iPhone screen.

Our first day, we walk around the Old Town and decide to take a two-hour river cruise. The boat is really an experience in itself, but in addition to the guided tour, it takes us to a little farm where we are served pineapple and watermelon and given several different fresh juices to sample. All the fruit is grown right there. It's very relaxing, and we meet some nice folks.

Because Chiang Mai is such a bargain, I hire a taxi ($50) for a day and go to the Elephant Conservation Camp, which I think everyone should do.

We watch the elephants being bathed, and we feed them bananas and sugar cane. We even feed a four-month-old baby elephant. I get in trouble for this, so remember—peel the bananas and break them up for the babies. The big elephants will eat a whole hand of bananas, peel and all. In my defense, I've never fed an elephant before.

We watch an elephant show where they demonstrate how elephants were used in the timber industry, and we watch the elephants paint pictures holding the brushes with their trunks. You can purchase the pictures after the show. We also ride an elephant for thirty minutes. This is a must-do, a once-in-a-lifetime experience. Part of the ride is through a river, as seen in the photo.

On the way home, we stop at several craft houses—we see how they carve rosewood and inlay mother of pearl, the girls paint small umbrellas at the umbrella factory, and we also take a quick look at a silver factory. Our driver stops at a local market along the road to show us different foods and plants. He buys us a sweet rice treat that is packaged in bamboo. He explains that bamboo has always been used as a container by the native people to prevent food from spoiling—very clever.

Another day we take an all-day cooking class, which is worth every penny (Chiang Mai Thai Cookery School). The kids are half price, they provide transportation to and from the school, and the cost is only $80 for all three of us. The facility is professional quality, and the chefs are well trained and very knowledgeable.

The cooking stations are outside. The classroom inside is state of the art with tiered seating and a huge mirror on the ceiling reflecting what's happening on the stove and on the counter. And, it's air conditioned, which provides a nice respite from the heat outside.

I learn how to hold a knife and the trick to peeling garlic quickly. Let's just say I'm not a great cook and never plan to be. But the cooking class is taught in a way that allows people at any level to learn something. All the ingredients are supplied to us washed and premeasured just like on TV cooking shows. If this happened at home, I might like to cook more.

We cook from a recipe book we get to keep, and our lunch is what we've cooked so far. Some people's lunches are better than others! I don't plan on making any of these dishes again because they're too complicated for me—more than six ingredients. But the girls could. We have a wonderful day and hang out with some nice people.

Rose gets a henna tattoo as does Ella at the Chiang Mai Sunday Market. This is our first henna experience. When we check out of the hotel, we not only pay for our room but also buy the hotel pillow cases and towels. Next time we'll know to wash the tattooed area before going to bed.

My biggest joy in Chiang Mai is the different markets. On this particular day, we buy hippie skirts and a dress for $2.50 each and handmade headbands for 50 cents, get thirty-minute foot massages for $2, eat sushi and all kinds of great street food for dinner, and get henna tattoos. We may have spent $25 total and have a blast.

On other days we shop, eat, and generally try to figure out this city. We particularly like eating at the restaurants along the river. I treat Rose and Ella to their first flambéed dessert. When things are so inexpensive comparatively, we have to live a little.

We fly through Bangkok on February 15 to Surat Thani on our way to Koh Pha Ngan. I didn't realize that once landing we would have to take a one-hour bus ride and then a three-hour boat ride with delays in between to get to the island. Oops! In my defense, I again planned this trip on my iPhone for the most part. I did use the hotel lobby computer to book the tickets and make the reservations. A fellow tourist I met in the lobby was advising me, and she never told me about all these modes of transportation. So, cut me some slack here.

When we finally arrive at 10 p.m., Milky Bay Resort upgrades us to a villa. It's a standalone A-frame structure consisting of one huge wonderful room with a huge bathroom. It has two king-size beds in separate areas, and the room is beautifully arranged with a sectional sofa and large flat-screen TV on the wall. Clean towels topped with fresh orchids are folded on the bottom of our beds.

The food at the resort's two outdoor restaurants is to die for. We only leave the resort one evening to experience the downtown food market, but other than that, we eat and drink at our resort. The fruit drinks are heavenly. Ella asks if she can have another coconut drink, and I tell her she can have as many as she wants as long as she doesn't make herself sick. Ain't life grand when things are affordable?

On February 20, we return to Bangkok for our final days in Thailand. We return to Beijing on February 22 by way of Manila. Yes, we are again trying to save a few bucks.

We arrive back in Beijing on the last day of Chinese New Year—the celebration goes on for fifteen days. Who says the Chinese don't know how to party? This day is a memory I hope never to forget. There are fireworks everywhere, and I mean everywhere all the time. In front and to the side of our building, they're setting off strings of crackers and the real deal, in the sky, fireworks and every kind of explosive in between.

From Rose and Ella's bedroom window, we watch several different full-blown fireworks displays in the distance. The fireworks go on all day up to midnight. Can I just say our Fourth of July fireworks are pathetic compared to this? I guess since the Chinese invented fireworks, they like them and they're good at setting them off. It's fun for the day, but I can't imagine fifteen days of this. TaoTao has been on homeopathic tranquilizers at the vet during our time away for this very reason.

Fifth Visa Trip: Who Knew South Korea Was So Great

The weather in Beijing is bearable and knowing that with our new visas we'll have to travel again in thirty days, we settle back into Beijing life. Thirty days evaporate with school and tutoring. Now, it's off to South Korea. Why South Korea, you may ask? Well, it's only a two-hour direct flight, which is relatively inexpensive. Plus, we've never been there.

Let's just say that again I planned this trip by iPhone. I have no idea that tensions between North and South Korea are at an all-time high and missiles could be flying while we're there. After booking the trip, I announce to my friends and family what our plans are, and they question how safe it is. I then do some searches on my phone (remember no Google in China) and decide against any tours of the DMZ while we're there, and I say a few silent prayers for peace.

We leave Beijing at 5 in the morning in a snowstorm. The night before brought botched cat boarding arrangements. Rose, Ella, and I can't leave TaoTao in an all-wire cage with a dog housed directly beneath her in the front window of a pet supply store. The final blow is when I ask the store owner about a litter box and he asks if I brought one.

This is the place that came highly recommended by a Chinese woman we met at the vet in our building. I even called this place and questioned them about their experience with cats before I made the reservation. I thought this might be the answer to our boarding problems. This place is only twenty to thirty minutes from our house, it's $2 a day, they speak some English, and it came recommended. All I can say is, the Chinese have readily adopted dogs but still know little about cats ... as pets.

But miracles do happen. So, we are at the recommended clueless boarding place that is beyond unacceptable. I am totally stressed out, Rose and Ella are being so good, and I have to pull myself together. I feel I could be on the brink of a breakdown. It's started to rain and it's getting dark. I'm beside myself wondering what to do with the cat. So, as a last-ditch effort, I call ICVS, which is about an hour away, to see if they are still open. They are, and the person we know answers the phone and says she'll stay open until we get there. Bless you, Mary.

The other part of the miracle is that when we finally get a taxi, which takes us a good forty-five minutes, Rose discovers the taxi driver lives in the same complex we do. This is a city of twenty million people, and we are a good twenty minutes from our apartment. Do you realize how unusual this is? So, he not only waits for us to drop TaoTao with the vet and takes us back to the apartment but also agrees to pick us up at 5 a.m. the next morning to take us to the airport. Rose and Ella arrange all this in Chinese, since our driver speaks no English.

When we wake to snow-covered roads, I realize what a miracle all this really is. There are no cars on the road, much less a taxi. We never would have made our flight if not for the mishap with the cat. I don't know what you've experienced, but it's always when I think everything is going against me that something truly miraculous happens. It does make me think someone, somewhere, somehow is watching over me.

We have little to no expectations about Seoul. Our only knowledge other than the newly purchased guidebook is the extremely popular Psy song about Gangnam, which we learn firsthand is a very trendy area of Seoul. I end up booking our hotel, the Artnoveau City, in Gangnam because there are no available hotels in the tourist area, it costs about $100 a night including breakfast, and comes well recommended on Expedia.

Rose and Ella at the Gangnam subway stop

It turns out to be a wonderful pick. The breakfast is almost inedible by Western standards, but everything else is great. Our room is an efficiency with kitchen appliances as you walk in, a washer/dryer combo (you know how excited that makes me), a small sitting room with a bedroom area you can close off with sliding rice paper doors, and there's a small, spotless, modern bathroom. The closet in the bedroom is so well thought out that I want one at home. The room is small, but it's so well organized, clean, and sleek, and with the small sitting area, we love coming back to it and just lounging.

Plus, the location turns out to be very convenient. The airport bus from Gimpo lets us off about four blocks from the hotel, which is a straight shot down the street.

The bus costs a total of $17 for the three of us. I recommend riding the bus into town because being above ground gives you a sense of Seoul. On the way back to the airport, we choose the subway, which costs a total of $4. The closest subway stop to our hotel is Gangnam. It's about two and a half blocks directly up the street. The subway is extremely easy to navigate, and we use it to get everywhere.

When we initially arrive at the airport, we know we aren't in China any more. The airport is immaculate. The bathrooms are spotless with Waldorf toilets—you know, Western toilets with built-in bidets and heated seats. When you walk in the stall and begin to shut the door, a light comes on. There is even toilet paper. We're NOT in China anymore. The bathrooms make us joyous. No joke—it's amazing what a nice, clean bathroom can do for your spirits. Rose and Ella use the restrooms first and insist I go. They say, "You're not going to believe the bathroom, Mom."

We board the airport bus, which has large, comfortable seats with seatbelts. There is even a sign saying, "Please fasten your seatbelt." We are definitely not in China anymore. We feel a sense of relief.

We're amazed at how clean Seoul is. Our only complaint is that they need more public trash cans, so we can help keep it clean. Well, the other complaint is that food is expensive—very expensive. But on the whole, we love Seoul.

We find the South Korean people to be very friendly and eager to speak English. People go out of their way for us; one lady even gives us a tour of restaurants in her car. Another woman leaves her job, escorts us to a nearby restaurant, and orders for us.

Here we are sitting on the heated floor (Koreans heat buildings under the floors, which makes sitting on the floor like sitting on a heating pad—talk about wonderful!) eating a traditional noodle soup.

Ella is pictured wearing a mask she just made at the Bukchon Traditional Culture Centre. I find a ton of craft activities for the girls in the Insa-dong and Bukchon areas. This all starts with the mention of the Dong-Lim Knot Workshop in the *Lonely Planet.* This is one of the last crafts we find and the least interesting, but it gets us to the area where we find doll making, mask painting, gold rubbings, great cafés, and traditional Korean houses—hanoks.

Ella and Rose on the main street with the Gyeongbokgung Palace in the background where you can watch the changing of the guard. The palace tours are in English several times a day and are very well done.

Ella and Rose making paper dolls

This is the amazing water walk in central Seoul with all kinds of fun surprises

Ella and Rose in traditional Korean wear
at the National Folk Museum

The National Folk Museum has a very hands-on kids' section, which I love. The kids are so engaged that I'm able to leave them and get a cup of coffee. Notice how big the dresses are at the bottom. This allows the heat from the floors to go up them and keep people warm. Genius! We also go on an English tour of the museum, which is fascinating—it covers everything from birth to weddings and burials.

In Seoul, what hits me in the face is what American and Western financing and influence can do. At the time of our visit, the Korean War has been over for sixty years exactly. I learn that most of the war was fought in Seoul and pretty much destroyed it. So, Seoul has become what it is in sixty years. If the North Korean people ever see Seoul, I believe they'll either be so angry that they'll demand new leaders or be so jealous that they'll try to destroy Seoul.

Seoul and Hong Kong are in such direct contrast to mainland China. Both flourish due to Western influence. What China could be today if not for the Cultural Revolution and such horrible leaders.

Travel in China: Jiangsu Province with Jenny

When I'm standing at the neighborhood bus stop with Jenny one day, I comment on the poster behind us with fields of yellow flowers and say, "I'd like to visit this area someday." Little do I know this is Jenny's home province—Jiangsu—just above Shanghai. Jenny makes elaborate plans, and the week after Jim arrives back in China, we are boarding the overnight train to Yang Zhou in Jiangsu Province.

I have to add a disclaimer to this section. Jenny and Simon planned this whole trip and paid for EVERYTHING. We never saw a ticket or knew the price of anything. Jenny was an incredible hostess, and I only wish I had as many friends so willing to open their lives to visitors and haul them around as she does. This being said, many times I have no idea where we are, much less the name of the place. So, bear with me. This is an incredible area, but sometimes there are pictures I want to share but have no caption.

The first stop on our tour is Yang Zhou. The city is somewhat quiet now, but it used to be very important due to its location on the Beijing-Hangzhou canal and the number of rich salt dealers living here. This is the place Marco Polo visited in 1282 and stayed for three years. Maybe because its food was as good then as it is now.

After taking the overnight train from Beijing, we're met at the station at the crack of dawn by four of Jenny's friends

The Foreigners Are in 709

in a large SUV. They take us to breakfast at Fu Chun Teahouse on Yang Zi Road. This is one of the best meals we have in China. The dumplings we're served as a first course—yes, it's breakfast and there's a first course—are huge and juicy. There's even a ritual to eating them. You need to have a spoon to catch the juice. More types of dumplings arrive along with other specialties. The whole meal is just a total gastronomical experience.

These are the incredible, juicy dumplings.

After this huge breakfast, the group breaks up and one of Jenny's friends takes us to a beautiful, historic park called Shou Xi Hu. Shou means "next to" in this context. So, the park name means "just next to West Lake" referencing West Lake in Hangzhou, which was deemed the premier lake in China.

There are two outstanding architectural structures in the park: The Five-Pavilion Bridge and the White Pagoda. The Five-Pavilion Bridge is also called Lotus Bridge, because the five pavilions are shaped like the five petals of a lotus flower. The White Pagoda is one of only two in China. The other one is in Bei Hai Park in Beijing.

We eat lunch at the university where Jenny's friend works. In the afternoon, we go to a street where the old-style shops have been recreated. But it's rainy, so we browse a little and head back to the car.

We then head to Qin Hu Resort, where we stay overnight. We spend one day at the resort and tour an old town where there are reenactments of how life used to be. We also tour a wetlands park and end up in a TV documentary. Nothing big. It just shows Jim and the girls in one of the tour boats. Jenny's friend who toured with us just happens to see it as he's watching TV one Saturday afternoon. He sends Jenny a copy, which she plays for us. What are the chances?

When we enter the old village, there's music playing, and mist (created from dry ice) covers the pond area. As the mist clears and a huge red rose blooms, a singer emerges from the blossom. It's quite beautiful and a little over the top.

On the third morning, another friend of Jenny's takes us to the Rapeseed Flower Park in Xing Hua County. This is where the picture was taken that I initially saw at the bus stop. Rapeseed is used to make canola oil, and it's abundant in this province even along the roadside.

As planned, the next day Jenny returns to Beijing and we board the train for Nanjing, where Simon arranges our accommodations and has his students act as our tour guides. The students couldn't be nicer, and we see some terrific sights.

Sixth Visa Trip: We Like Japan, But ...

It's late April and our last trip out of Mainland China is to Japan. Remember, Jim lived here as a little boy. He's excited to be back. However, Japan isn't quite what I thought it would be. We have a great time on this trip and see a lot of interesting things, but it's not as clean, modern or technologically advanced as I thought it would be. After Seoul, I thought Japan would be even more advanced ... not so. When I say this to Jim, he reasons that Japan's infrastructure is older and it's showing its age as compared to Seoul, which was rebuilt so recently.

On our first morning in Tokyo, we head straight for the famed fish market. Our bags have been lost and will show up at our hotel later, which turns out to be ideal because it frees us from either going to the hotel immediately or dragging our stuff around all day.

The fish market is like a show of every sea creature you've ever seen and then multiplied exponentially. There are so many strange, colorful, oddly shaped creatures. It's a smorgasbord for the eyes.

In the picture above, Ella and Rose are giving their opinions on the fish heads in the bucket. There are lots of fish heads and other sea animal parts, but there isn't any odor. Maybe in the summer it's bad, but on the day we go, it's just a feast for the eyes. Everything seems to be organized, and the cleanliness of the entire place is striking. Imagining how all the business transactions work boggles my mind.

We grab a sushi snack at one of the hole-in-the-wall places along the market that the guidebook recommends. It's so small that we separate to be seated. Rose and I eat at the counter.

The picture above shows the beginning of our treat. We order the set menu because I don't know enough about sushi to order anything else. It's expensive at $35. We don't know what we're eating but find out later that one thing is sea urchin roe, which I swear tastes like pumpkin pie filling.

After the fish market, we walk to the Hama-Rikyu Gardens. The trees are unbelievably sculpted. The shadows they cast are like Chinese paper cuts. Truly works of art.

We stop in at the garden tea house and sample the Matcha, which is a powdered green tea mixed with hot water. It's in the bowl to the right. The sweet, to the left, is cut with the wooden stick shown. I think both are an acquired taste.

The next day, for our fifteenth wedding anniversary, we SPLURGE and have lunch at BEIGE. Rose and Ella are pictured pointing out the "somewhat" subtle restaurant logo by the elevator we take to the top floor where the restaurant is housed. Beige is a collaboration between Chanel and a famous French chef, Alain Ducasse.

Can you say expensive? Try $600 for lunch. Jim had the menu with the prices, and I thought it was a set $50/person meal. The guidebook misled us a little on price.

We aren't dressed appropriately and get seated away from the crowd at a corner table on the upper level of the restaurant by ourselves. However, I really like this set-up. It gives us a great vantage point to people watch. I spy someone hosting a baby shower. Can you imagine the cost of that?

Jim and Rose at Beige

I had pictures of our meal but in grayscale it doesn't look appetizing. So, here's the menu:

Bread—a slice and a roll—fresh
White fish with a tomato cream sauce
Lobster, of course
Veggies in a pureed pea sauce—It's unexpectantly good
Kobe beef—oh, so good
Macaroons—grapefruit and green tea
Jim's dessert—sponge cake with brandy

So, we splurge on lunch and stay in a cage. This is Kimi Ryokan, where we sleep on the floor and share a hall bath.

This is the entrance to our room—209. Behind the cage door is another sliding door that locks with a key.

Of course, Jim booked this. In his defense, a ryokan is a traditional Japanese inn that typically features tatami matted rooms with communal baths. We're participating in a Japanese cultural experience. Whatever.

Here's Ella wearing the supplied yukata inside the room with the tatami bedding shown behind her.

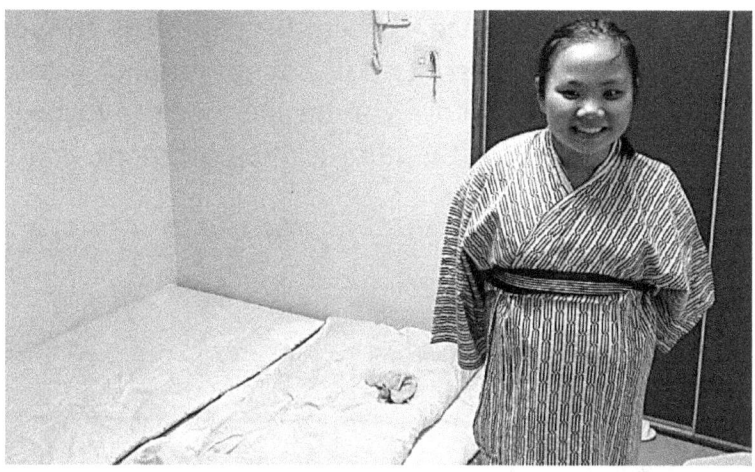

This is hilarious. The guide book goes on and on about this fabulous oak bath everyone must try. I thought the tub was for a group hot-tub experience. So, the girls and I give it a try.

I'm now pretty sure it's a one-person thing. I could go on about how ridiculous the three of us are trying to share this small tub, but I won't. Just imagine having three people in your bathtub at home.

If you want to experience it, there's a shower in the room. Do all your cleaning there and just enjoy the hot water after, if you choose. Before you decide, see the following notice that's posted on the door of the bathroom.

For the record, we were the first ones in, and yes, we drained it. I couldn't help myself.

Udon noodles are top choices on Rose and Ella's list of favorite foods no matter the meal. And, yes, in China and Japan you can drink from the bowl. Don't know how we're going to break this habit once we get home.

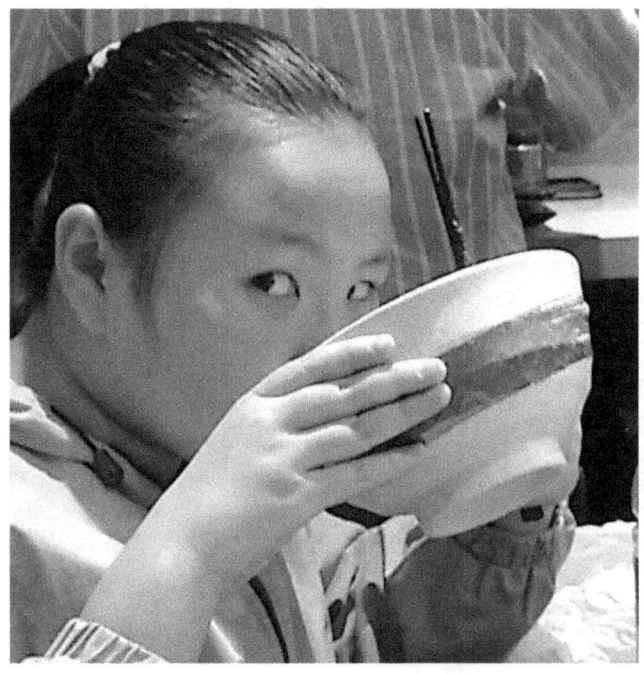

The Foreigners Are in 709

Displaying replicas of a restaurant's fare is quite common in Japanese restaurant windows. I think it's an art form, simply beautiful.

OK, we have checked out of the Ryokan and aren't sleeping on the floor tonight but … We are now checked into the E Hotel also in Tokyo. Want to know what the E stands for? I believe eensy-weensy. Again, we may splurge on food but not on accommodations.

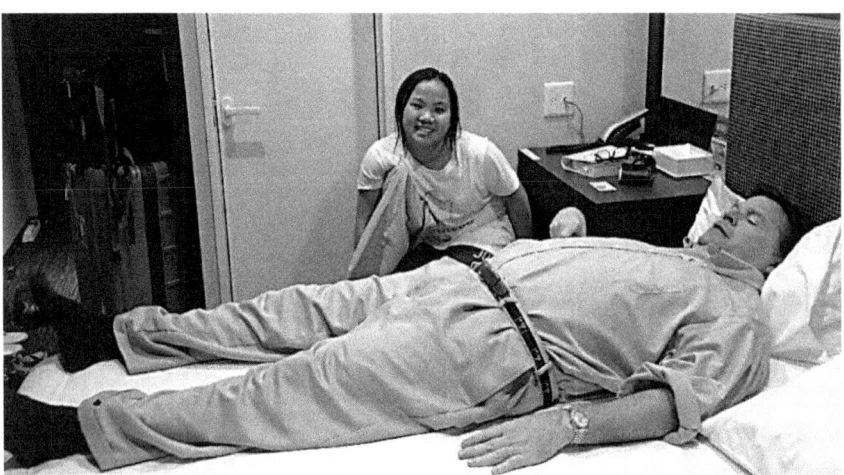

I've never been in a room this small. In fact, I've been in bigger closets. But the bathroom takes the prize. It's just behind where Ella's sitting. Think of an airplane restroom, but in that same space there's also a bathtub. Mind you, the tub is a soaking tub, but there's still a tub. The sink faucet doubles as the tub faucet—I'm NOT kidding. I do take a bath because this is so incredible that I want to say I did it. Jim marvels that they can fit so much technology in such a small space. I marvel that he can fit.

Thank God for the room's window. In one hotel, they gave us a room without a window. That lasted as long as it took me to run back to the front desk. After getting over my claustrophobic feelings of this room, I do notice how clean it is. We also find a great sushi bar across the street where we hang out and drink lots of sake, returning to the room only to sleep.

OMG. Mt. Fuji is breathtaking. When I first spot it, all I can say is, "Oh, my God."

From Tokyo, we take a bus to Mt. Fuji's 5th Station. The 5th Station is the highest point you can get to by road, and it has opened just a few days before our arrival. It's a beautiful day, and Mt. Fuji looms over creation.

July and August are the months you can hike Mt. Fuji without snow gear. Since we're in jeans, we just window-shop and walk a short distance on a couple of the trails. We're lucky there aren't more people here. We've arrived during Golden Week, when most of Japan takes a ten-day vacation.

The 5th Station has some shops, restaurants, shrines, and trails. It reminds me of a ski resort.

This is near the shrine, and I just think
Ella and Rose look cute here.

After looking around, eating and hiking a bit, we take another bus to the lake town at the base of Mt. Fuji where we're staying at a hostel.

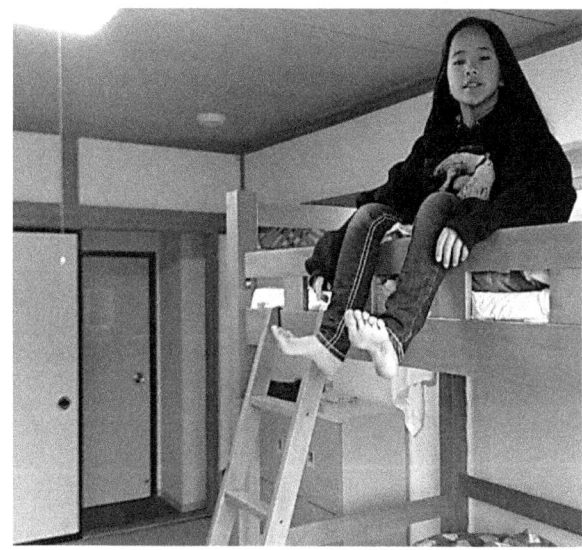

Rose has the top bunk, and I have the one under her. If you're going to stay in a hostel, Japan is a good place to do it. It's a good deal at 2,500 yen per night. With the exchange rate being 100 yen to the dollar, it costs $25 per person.

K's House Mt. Fuji is immaculate, and the staff is exactly what you want when you travel. They make sightseeing recommendations, eating suggestions, and travel arrangements, and they're friendly. Plus, K's provides a van to transport you to your next mode of transportation.

The facility itself is nice. The common room is a good size, and so is the kitchen. The girls and I watch *Beethoven,* the dog movie, in the common area before we go out to a traditional Hutu restaurant whose menu is heavy on horse meat. We say "neigh" to this (sorry, I couldn't resist.) and move on to the noodle section of the menu.

Our room arrangement is very interesting. You saw in the other picture that Rose and I have bunks on the opposite wall. This picture shows Ella getting down from her top bunk and Jim lying on his bottom bunk against this wall.

The mind wanders to the fact that there is yet another set of bunks. Come to find out, there were no Japanese-style family rooms available when Jim booked this accommodation several weeks earlier. We're in the six-bed mixed dormitory. Do I need to tell you it slipped Jim's mind to tell me this? Jim says to remember BEIGE. All I see is red.

So, who's sleeping in the bunks adjacent to Jim and Ella? There's what looks like a big purse on the top bunk, and the bottom bunk is unclaimed. I won't hold you in too much suspense. The "purse" belongs to a man from Thailand who wears matching pajamas, and I suspect his mommy packed his teddy bear, too. The bottom bunk goes to a nice thirtyish Canadian man who is teaching in Shanghai.

Everyone but Mr. Thailand sleeps pretty much fully dressed. It's a little weird lying in bed talking to a young Canadian man while my husband and children are right there, but he's interesting and I like him. All I can say is, from an American woman's perspective, sharing a room with two unknown men seems very weird in the beginning, but once you get acquainted, it's not so bad. I'd do it again.

K's isn't fancy, but it's very comfortable. Staying at communal accommodations always forces us to talk and interact with a lot of travelers, which I think enhances the trip. On previous occasions, we've gotten great travel tips and we've met lots of interesting people. It's usually a little uncomfortable at first, but I think it adds to the fun and surprise of travel.

Getting from Mt. Fuji to Kyoto is a bit cumbersome and expensive. I recommend getting a JR pass for the trains before you leave the U.S. if you plan to spend much time in Japan. We take a very nice bus to Mishima. The bus lets us off at the train station, where we eat lunch and take a fast train to Kyoto.

Again, I have to admit, I don't know where we are half the time in Kyoto because Jim's leading the way and I'm taking it easy. So, a lot of these pictures are uncaptioned because I have no idea at this point exactly where we are but they're too pretty to leave out.

The Foreigners Are in 709

Ella, Rose, and Jim are taking the waters for longevity.

The Monkey Park is a big hit with all of us. This is a must-do. It's a steep climb at points but well worth it. Just keep telling yourself that and you'll make it. Part way up, you start to see the monkeys and you forget the climb.

It's spring, so we get to see lots of baby monkeys, and the climb is easier with the cooler weather.

The monkeys get very close.

Once you get to the top, there is a panoramic view of Kyoto.

Here's a monkey hanging on the side of the feeding house waiting for a handout. You can buy apple slices and peanuts in the shell for a dollar a bag. The monkeys shell the peanuts before eating them, just like we do. You hold the food in your hand with fingers extended straight. The monkeys reach their little hands through the screen and gently take the food. It's an amazing feeling.

From Kyoto, we take the fast train to Tokyo. Outside the train station, the black cars waiting are taxis. They are very clean (inside and out), and the drivers wear white gloves. It's like being chauffeured. The meter starts at around $7, whereas in Beijing it's $1.66. Needless to say, transportation in Japan is a bit costlier than we're accustomed to, but it's done in style.

The interior of the Tokyo train station is super modern, super clean, and has great restaurants and high-end shopping.

In Tokyo, we take the monorail to Odaiba Island. It's a very futuristic ride and provides incredible views of Tokyo and the ocean.

On the island, we go to an onsen—Japanese bath. Jim and the girls are pictured at the entrance with Big Blue, our suitcase. We won't check in to our airport hotel until late tonight.

Pictured are Rose and Ella in their onsen-supplied yukatas in the entertainment area. After walking in the therapeutic river bed, having the dead skin on their feet nibbled off by little fish, cleaning and showering, and soaking nude in the hot tubs, it's time for live entertainment, food, and carnivalesque activities. Yes, everyone is wearing a robe, not just us.

Jim and I have sake, and we all get sushi and tempura as snacks. We make ourselves comfortable on the floor and watch the live entertainment. The funniest thing is the man playing the recorder with his nose—not his mouth. This makes me think I shouldn't correct my children so much. Who knows, maybe they could make a living doing some of the weird and disgusting things they do. I mean, look at Jim Carrey. After this, we peruse the carnival games and eat dinner.

All in all, it's a very interesting experience. With the nudity part and being the uber parent that I am, I try for a teaching moment. As we're sitting nude in a hot tub with more than one hundred other nude women soaking and meandering around, I say to the girls, "Don't ever worry about your body—as you can see, people come in all shapes and sizes." Their response, "This is weird."

Jim and I are very much out of our comfort zone with the onsen thing when this all starts, but as afternoon turns to evening, we think it's an incredible cultural experience. You should try it—when you enter the onsen, you register as you would in a hotel. In fact, there is a hotel component to this onsen. As you check in, everyone who is going on your bill is given a wrist band that you use to buy whatever you want. All your personal belongings, including wallets, are put in a locker for safe keeping. The girls are pictured getting ready to order dinner and will pay by using the bands. When we get the bill at the end of the night, we're a bit surprised, but the whole experience is so worth the splurge. It's a whole day and evening of entertainment.

Here we are in the entertainment area in our robes.

The Foreigners Are in 709

In the tatami room, you eat and drink sitting on the floor. Then, if you want to relax or go to sleep, it's perfectly acceptable to fall back, stretch out and make yourself comfy. After stuffing yourself, doesn't everyone want to do this? What a great custom. This onsen is only closed from 9 to 11 a.m., so you can stay all night if you want.

Here's the official way to wear a yukata. There's great signage everywhere to let you know what to do when. Some of us were better than others at finding and reading them. We had to send Jim back to get his underwear once.

An American family livin' the life in China

Marathon to Know Everything
Beijing, May 4 – July 1

Mutianyu (The Great Wall of China)

Back in Beijing, we want to go to the Great Wall again. There are several public places to experience the Great Wall in Beijing. Two of the most popular are Badaling, in northwest Beijing, and Mutianyu, in the northeast. Reagan went to Badaling; Clinton to Mutianyu. The Youngs have already been to Badaling several times this trip and now want to see Mutianyu.

My interest in Mutianyu started early on. When we were staying at the Holiday Inn before finding our apartment, I had a conversation with a Chinese woman in the hotel elevator about her trip to the Great Wall. She highly recommended Mutianyu. We'd also seen a great Thanksgiving overnight experience advertised in *The Beijinger* for the School House Restaurant at Mutianyu.

But for some reason I can't remember, the Thanksgiving trip didn't work out.

So, we randomly choose this weekend. We pick up the kids at 1 p.m. from school and take Subway Line Four to Subway Line Two to Dongzhimen station. Then, we go around the corner to a bus station in the building. (We discover on the way back that you can also get to the bus through the subway tunnels.) There we catch Express Bus 916 to Huairou, which takes about an hour and fifteen minutes. Here's the tricky part: You get off the bus, cross the road and get on a different 916 bus that takes you to Mutianyu. This whole bus ride with our transit cards costs about $2 each.

To our amazement, the bus stop where we get off is right across the road from our hotel—Xin Shuang Quan Resort. It's a sustainable hotel (not a resort by any stretch of the imagination). This concept is a little different for us, making us a little apprehensive but we're very pleased with our room. We have them add an extra bed for 200 yuan for a total price for the room running around $100. It's a bit expensive for where we are and what we get, but what can we do?

The eating area and lobby are quite extensive and weird. They are set up to seat at least five hundred for meals, but it's only us and the staff. It's very reminiscent of our Mongolian accommodations, but our room is cool with exposed brick and it's very clean.

After getting ourselves checked in and settled, we take a twenty-minute hike up the road toward the Great Wall to the School House Restaurant, which sounded great from all we had read. However, our expectations aren't met. Jim and I order hamburgers, which cost about $20 each but are mediocre at best.

On the positive side, the girls like their pasta dishes and we're able to sit outside and enjoy a foggy view of the Great Wall. All in all, we spend about a $100 on a so-so meal with poor service, but I'm not sure there was anything any better—maybe cheaper.

The next morning, we get a ride from the hotel up the hill to the wall entrance costing fifty yuan—which should have cost ten at the most. Oh well, this seems to be the trend in this town.

We could spend more cash on souvenirs. There's about two blocks worth of wall-to-wall vendors. I hate to admit it, but over the course of the year, we've purchased just about everything they offer. But because it's a bit nippy, I do find an "I climbed up the Great Wall" sweat shirt to help stimulate the economy. I'm very proud to say that after honing my bargaining skills over the past year, I get it for $5. After my conquest, we ride the chairlift to the wall (you can walk but you're going to do a lot of walking once you're on the wall. There's also a cable car you can take.).

The fog is scheduled to lift at 1 p.m., according to the Weather Channel app on my iPhone. This doesn't happen, but we don't get hot either. We like this section of the wall. It isn't as crowded as Badaling, and the steps are pretty much a consistent height, making it easier to climb.

If you haven't been to the wall, mentally have a hike in mind, not a saunter.

Ella and Rose on the wall.

Yes, there are food and drink vendors on the wall. You can even sip a beer, but there's no bathroom.

Some views are just beautiful.

The man with his shirt hiked up is so Chinese. You see this look everywhere as soon as it starts to get warm.

Just to let you know, I left Beijing with the equivalent of $300 in my pocket, which I thought was overkill. But with the prices being much higher than I expected and there being a problem with my credit card, funds are running low even before we make it up the hill to the wall. The good news is, there's an ATM just to the left of the wall entrance near the chairlift. The transportation up and back for the four of us costs about $50.

The part of the wall Ella enjoys the most is the luge ride down. You sit on a sled on a half tube slide. There are warnings at the start not to do this if you have heart problems! Rose and I aren't so sure about this and choose to ride together, which turns out to be quite fun and not as dangerous as I had thought.

Now, if you have that beer or the ride down upsets your stomach, there are public restrooms at the base of the wall. I like the signage for the squat toilet.

Family Weekend Excursions

I want to make sure I see most everything in Beijing that the guidebooks and English magazines talk about. You know, I can't have lived here for a year and have someone say, "Did you see the such and such?" and say, "No, where is that?" I'm a little crazed about this.

Anyway, in my frenzy, I run across a treasure hunt in the *Time Out Beijing* magazine for April (this is another English expat magazine). One of the hunts includes the Lama Temple (Yonghegong—Subway Line Two), the Confucius Temple, Samantha Crafts (I meet Samantha), and Fancy Massage and Nails, among other sites. I go to this area several days to poke around the shops and get a massage and pedicure.

I've been looking for ages for a Hutong street named Nanluoguxiang that all the magazines talk about. One of the hunts includes it and the new Subway Line Six even has a stop by the same name. I'm so excited by this I can hardly stand it. This is a brand-new subway line, and it opens a whole new area for me to explore.

What a find this is. I have finally found the cool part of Beijing. It reminds Jim and me of the French Concession area of Shanghai, but not quite as interesting. I've been skirting this area for months while exploring the lakes just west of the Forbidden City. I find it all connects.

The lake area has wonderful rooftop cafés, where you can watch the action on the street and lake, although these restaurants usually cost a fortune. You also know you're in a touristy area when you see the rickshaws. Hold onto your wallet.

The Foreigners Are in 709

Anyone for donkey? Yes, they do eat donkey here. This restaurant is near the Nanluoguxiang subway stop. Even though Rose is standing in front, we don't enter.

Mother's Day Weekend—TRB And Zhongshan Park

The weather has been in the 80s for the past week, and we've had blue sky days all weekend. We visit Yonghegong, aka the Lama Temple, on Saturday. There is a subway stop by the same name on Line Two, which makes it easy to find. According to the guidebook, the Lama Temple is the largest and best-preserved lamasery in Beijing. It was built in 1694 and was initially the residence of Prince Yongzheng before he ascended the throne. In 1744, it was converted into a lamasery for lamas from Mongolia and Tibet. There are literally hundreds of Buddhas of all shapes and sizes housed here. Plus, the area around it is a neat shopping experience.

This is a statue of Tsongkhapa, the founder of Lamaism. It's housed in the Hall of the Wheel of Law, where lamas read scripture and Buddhist ceremonies are still conducted. Note the study lamps.

This is one of the many incense burners outside the buildings comprising the lamasery. It's a windy day and there are signs saying not to light incense, but in typical Chinese fashion, incense burns freely.

This is the last of the buildings in this complex. It's called the Pavilion of Boundless Happiness. I love this name.

It is made up of a three-story building flanked by two-story buildings. They are linked on either side by a sky corridor. Housed in the three-story portion is the fifty-five-meter sandalwood statue of the Maitreya Buddha. There's no picture of this because I finally see the no-photo sign. Oops! You'll have to take my word on this—the architectural details and colors are just amazing.

On Sunday, I teach my class and with Rose's help, we make Mother's Day cards and crepe paper flowers for the kids to give their moms. Mother's Day is not celebrated in China, or maybe it's like Valentine's Day—not celebrated on the same day as we celebrate it.

After class, we meet Ella and Jim for lunch at TRB, Temple Restaurant Beijing. This is an amazing restaurant in a restored old temple and courtyard buried in winding streets near the north entrance of the Forbidden City. Remember, we know this restaurant because Jim and the girls met one of the owners in the hot tub in Taiwan. We dropped his name the last time Jim and I were here, and this time we get a window, corner, primo table. It's the type of restaurant where the owner remembers you and comments on the last time you were here.

After lunch, we walk to Jingshan Park, which is across from the northern gate of the Forbidden City. This area is the center of Beijing. The park was once an imperial garden during the Ming and Qing Dynasties (1368—1911). It used to be the highest point in the city and still provides great views. This is a must-see attraction that most people miss, but it's so accessible, and the cultural insights gained from any park experience are tremendous.

Okay, so maybe it's a little touristy. We take this picture of us dressed as the Chinese royal family at the top of Jingshan Park.

It costs 40 yuan ($6.66). To see Jim in this get-up—priceless. Nice beads! Plus, how many more years will the girls let me get away with things like this? I'm already getting, "This is so embarrassing." It does make me think twice about the ridiculousness of this as I watch other people taking our picture. Maybe I should be embarrassed? But it makes the perfect Christmas card—I just couldn't help myself.

The park is quite a beautiful spot. At times, a feeling of what it must have been like during the Qing and Ming Dynasties can almost be grasped. Then, about fifteen hundred tourists walk in front of you and you're back to reality.

This is the view from the top looking to the south with the Forbidden City in the foreground and modern Beijing in the background. Our apartment is out there somewhere in the distance.

This is a side profile of the blue-haired Buddha. The blue-haired Buddha sits inside the open-air pavilion at the top. The blue symbolizes heaven.

This is one of the two pavilions in the park—lovely!

The Foreigners Are in 709

The view to the left is Beihai Park with its White Dagoba towering above the other buildings. The White Dagoba was built in 1651 in honor of the visiting Dalai Lama. To the right, you can see the mountains where the Summer Palace is located.

When we hike down the other side of the hill, we see a musician accompanied by a soloist with bystanders dancing to the music. This is quite a common scene in Chinese parks. Although, I've never thought of the Chinese as accordion players, this man is quite good.

The peonies are in full bloom, and an art class is in session.

Pizza Hut, Prince Gongs Mansion, and More

We are tired of Chinese food. With the bird flu, being told the kabobs are possibly cat or rat soaked in lamb urine and being told not to eat other foods because of possible chemical contamination, we are very happy to find a Pizza Hut we can walk to—thirty minutes away. It's two stories of pure bliss. It's clean. The pizza tastes just like home, and they have half-off specials every day. I would usually frown on this, but I miss home and my food. I've been a very good sport for the most part, but all of us have pretty much had it with eating foreign food.

The Foreigners Are in 709

Rose and Ella at our neighborhood Pizza Hut.

Cheating on the food doesn't mean I've given up on my quest to see the little-known sightseeing treasures that grab my attention. So, as a family, we go to Prince Gong's Residence near Beihai Lake on June 1. It's huge, in the cool part of town, and well worth seeing. However, don't go with someone whose feet hurt and is a whiner. You'll notice most pictures are of Rose, who is a trooper.

When Jim mentions our last month or so in China, he says we visited things even the Chinese who live in Beijing never see. He says we not only see first- and second-tier sights but third-tier ones as well. He's right, Jenny almost joined us to see Prince Gong's because she's never been. But, I think Jim should stop complaining, buy some comfortable shoes, and join me on my quest with a smile on his face. I'm not dissuaded.

So, here's Prince Gong's Palace. There are many, many buildings, shrines, and interesting signage.

An American family livin' the life in China

The "Fu" Stele (Fu Zi Bei)

The big Chinese character "Fu" (implying blessing) inscribed on the stele is the personal handwriting of Emperor Kangxi(r.1662—1722) of the Qing Dynasty.

After leaving Prince Gong's, we head over to Nanluoguxiang. Rose negotiates a great rate for this ride, and we all pile on.

The following pictures are of Nanluoguxiang. This is the truly cool area of town along with the lake area. There are trendy, one-of-a-kind restaurants and shops snuggled in this ancient area of town. It's artsy and fun but maybe a little overdone. Jenny tells me this is a big tourist area. Well, it is for the Chinese. There is an abundance of Chinese tourists here but not so many white folks. So, it still feels like a find to me.

The contraption we ride in drops us off here at the north entrance of the street right in front of the man pictured above. He's making a craft I saw at the beginning of our trip near The Temple of Heaven and have wanted the girls to see. The man takes a caramel gooey substance and blows it like glass. Ella has him make a horse for her, since her birth was in the year of the horse. It's really neat to watch. Just don't eat it. It tastes bad and the man has spit in it.

Glasses with no lenses are quite the craze in China right now. I find it hard to take adults seriously when they're wearing these. Again, this is something I just shake my head at. My children join the fashion craze.

Jim planned a musical evening for us months ago. He bought tickets to hear the Beijing Symphony Orchestra in the Forbidden City Concert Hall for June 8. It's a great deal—30 yuan or $5/ticket. So, tonight's the night. The venue is nice, and it's in Zhongshan Park just to the left of the Forbidden City's southern entrance. So, at the end of the concert, we are filled with the music and we stroll through the park on the way to the subway. It's a lovely experience.

However, Ella has been sick with a fever for the past four days. We decide to leave Ella and Rose at home alone. This is the first time we have ever left the girls at home alone for any length of time. We call Simon and Jenny to give them a heads-up, and Jim coaches the girls on what to do in case of any type of emergency—call Jenny. I just hope they won't fight among themselves and need medical help. The girls are asleep when we get home—no obvious signs of bloodshed.

The next day is a rainy Saturday. Ella has no fever, so we venture to the National Museum of China on Tiananmen Square. Admission is free, but you have to show your passport. We skip around based on Jim's Chinese dialogue he just studied and see a lot of cool things.

The girls and I toured part of the museum and ate at the café in the dead of winter, but I'm glad to return because there's so much more to see. Plus, Jim and I have been debating whether to go to Xian to see the terra cotta warriors or go to Yunnan to see beautiful scenery. We decide on Yunnan. So, I love seeing the museum's display of the terra cotta soldiers and horses. This way, we've seen them without going to Xian. Check that off the list.

Jim hasn't been to the Olympic Village, and the girls really want to go to the water park at the Water Cube. It's highly recommended as a kids' activity in *The Beijinger*. I think this is a great idea. How many people can say they have swum where Olympians have?

When we get there, the grounds of the Olympic Village are packed with Chinese tourists and vendors. This is a huge space, and there are lots of people.

The price to enter the Cube is pretty steep—adults 200 yuan ($33) and kids 160 yuan ($26). I only go in as an observer and it's 30 yuan ($5). I think admission has to be high or the Cube would be even more packed. The kids have a blast. Jim has an OK time. He thinks the locker room needs some upgrades.

Jim, Rose, and Ella in front of the Bird's Nest

Jim and the girls are allowed in at 5 p.m. and stay until just before 8.

At 8, we grab some hot dogs and soup for dinner at a fast-food place on the second floor, where I've been sitting overlooking the whole water park. The food is awful, but to see the Cube and the Bird's Nest lit up at night is worth coming at night. Plus, when I have the girls independently write their top ten things about our trip to China, the Water Cube makes the top of both lists.

The Olympic pool inside the Water Cube

Note the rings on this man's back. I saw these on people on the subway when we first arrived in Beijing and thought there was a horrible outbreak of ring worm in China. Come to find out, it's just from cupping. Also, note the addiction to the cell phone. Cell phones are everywhere, and everyone has one.

This is a section of the water park inside the Cube. Several people don't go through the tube on the left fast enough and get stuck at the bottom. There's a trap door to get them out. It happens several times while we are there. It's a little dangerous but kind of funny.

The Bird's Nest and Cube at night

Here we are pictured in front of where the Chinese Congress meets in Tiananmen Square. Jim decides to join me today on my quest to see everything. Our overall goal today is to find where the president of China lives. We are checking this out while the girls are in school to see if it's worth a weekend excursion.

Yes, it's mid-June and the girls are still in school. No one has yet given us a definitive date for the last day. We think it might be July 13. (We learn later it's July 10.) This has been a trend. When we originally met with the school and paid tuition, I asked for the school calendar. "Yes, yes, we will get you one." This is so Chinese. The Chinese are very accommodating and never tell you that what you're requesting or what you want is not available. Remember Rose's birthday cake?

We think not providing the school holiday dates until a few days prior to when they happen is a means of Communist control. It makes it very difficult to plan your life when you don't know when you're supposed to send the kids to school or you're supposed to work. Businesses and schools follow the same holiday schedule.

Several times during the year we are told the week before that everyone will work and go to school through the weekend and then will be given the following Monday, Tuesday and Wednesday off as holidays. Where else in the world would anyone do this and a whole country comply? Again, I shake my head. My Chinese friends accept this practice and seem puzzled as to why I question it. This is not normal to me, but it goes to show, if you've never known anything different, it's normal.

Back to sightseeing. From the Congressional building, we walk up the street. Looking beyond Tiananmen Square and Chang'an Jie (one of the main thoroughfares in Beijing) we see Tiananmen Rostrum with Mao's portrait. This is the entrance to the Forbidden City. (Whenever you see "men" at the end of a Chinese word it usually means gate. These ancient cities were built as fortresses with walls encircling them for protection and gates for entrance.) For centuries, this gate area was used for important ceremonies such as enthronements and sending armies off to battle.

The colorful columns and spheres in the foreground of the picture show a creativity that contrasts sharply with the bland Soviet-inspired architecture of Tiananmen Square but prepares you for the amazing color combinations and architecture of the Forbidden City.

As I mentioned, Jim and I are trying to find where the president of China lives. My tour book, *Travel in Beijing,* says he lives on the southern-most lake, Zhongnanhai, just to the west of the Forbidden City. The book says this area has been home to the highest-ranking members of the Communist Party, including Mao, since the founding of the People's Republic of China in 1949. This book, written in 2006, says Chairman Mao's former residence and several other sites in this south lake area are open to the public every Saturday and Sunday. It suggests you enter by a gate at 81 Nanchang Street. I quote, "The mysterious land is now easily accessible."

Well, not any more folks. Jim and I try the suggested address and every street corner thereafter and before for several blocks. We are approached by uniformed, armed guards who speak little or no English, but it's clearly understood that this area is totally off limits regardless of the day of the week.

Travel in China: Yunnan Province

Why Yunnan? Because *Lonely Planet* says, "If you have time to visit only one province in China, then it should be Yunnan." To book our flights and hotels, I use the Ctrip travel site, which all works fairly well. However, my privilege to book our family trips may be revoked. I'm accumulating some iffy experiences—not horrible, but on the verge. Lesson here is that Jim is a great trip planner and should always do it.

Here's a synopsis of pitfalls with me being the planner. As you may remember, the trip to Koh Pha Ngan, Thailand, was based solely on a single conversation with a woman I had just met in the hotel lobby. This caused us to lose two vacation days. Let's just say next time I'll fly to a closer airport and not spend an additional six to eight hours getting to our destination. Then, I book our trip to South Korea at a time when "relations between North and South Korea have never been worse since the end of the Korean War sixty years ago." OK, I was working solely from my iPhone then and had no other access to media.

On our current trip, all I can say is that it's becoming obvious that I'm challenged with transportation between cities. But in all fairness, shouldn't the guidebooks have given me a heads-up? OK, maybe when the two-hour train from Dali to Lijiang is sold out, I should have checked other train reservations. Because of this, we end up on a three-and-a-half-hour, terrifying bus ride where I get to ride shotgun and see everything coming straight for us.

But, this is where I really mess up. On our final leg from Lijiang back to Kunming, the train sleepers are sold out. We have a flight to catch the next day—we must get back. So, we end up with three hard seats and one standing ticket for a ten-hour overnight train ride. Did I mention these seats aren't together? They're in the same car and we do manage to get two together after making some trades. This gives Rose, Ella and me two seats among us. For a while, it's fine, but as we want to sleep, the three of us are uncomfortable and the girls are tired and crying. I'm a failure as a trip planner and as a mother, but they finally fall asleep. Fast-forward several days to when we're all home and it makes a good story. One I hope NEVER to repeat. Lesson learned here is to book the train tickets as far in advance as possible, especially during the summer months.

Here are the three of us at the beginning of the trip sharing two seats. We're still smiling. There are three high school students across from us and one beside me sharing a seat with an old man who has a standing ticket. The high school student eventually joins her friends on the other side, leaving me straddling the seat hump of the third seat with the old man at my side.

Here are the vitals of this trip. We're in Yunnan between June 12 and 18, 2013. It's a three-and-a-half-hour flight from Beijing to Kunming. From Kunming, we go north to Dali and Lijiang. Then, from Lijiang we travel back to Kunming where we fly back to Beijing.

Our hotel in Kunming is the Jin Jiang Hotel—$90/night including one breakfast; additional breakfasts are 50 yuan ($8). At one time, this was a top hotel, but not anymore. The hotel is worn. However, the location is a huge benefit— the airport bus stops here (25 yuan/person ($4), and it's near the train station. When we arrive back in Kunming from Lijiang, we know to return to the hotel parking lot to purchase our bus tickets and catch the airport bus. This is a blessing after our less-than-perfect sleeping arrangements.

In Dali, we stay at the Yinfeng Hotel for $30/night. I strongly recommend this motel. It's new and clean, and the staff and location are great. We have a sitting room and a huge bathroom with lots of hot water.

In Lijiang, we stay at the Dongba Hotel Lijiang Old Town. This is a great place. It's $30/night and an extra 50 Yuan ($8) for the kids. This includes a Western breakfast, which is ample and delicious. Ella ends up sleeping on the sofa and has a great night's sleep.

What makes this place so ideal is that it is built around a courtyard where we have breakfast, talk to the other guests, and play with the dogs, puppy and turtle. There is another breakfast room with two computers and another outdoor space where they have a traditional tea service in the afternoon. One of the managers, Joyce, speaks perfect English and helps us with everything, including booking our train tickets online with her own credit card and the hotel's account number.

Our trip to Yunnan gets off to a good start. We get to the airport a bit early and have fun playing with the plyboard cut-outs of flight attendants.

Me, hanging with my Miao minority group pals in the Beijing airport. According to *Lonely Planet,* more than half of China's ethnic groups are from Yunnan.

This is Green Lake Park. It's in a great section of Kunming with wonderful little cafés and shops on the streets surrounding it.

This photo is taken from the hotel restaurant on the twenty-third floor and gives a panoramic view of the thriving city.

We spend several hours at the Yunnan Nationalities Museum. Among other things, the museum has a very interesting clothing exhibit. The outfit on the far left is made from tree bark, and the other two are made from straw. Seems a little scratchy to me.

Here's a bamboo house of the Dai minority

The four-and-a-half-hour bus ride from Kunming to Dali is incredibly beautiful. A lot of the hillsides are terraced. On many hilltops there are wind turbines, one after the other, for miles.

The exterior stairs of our hotel lead to the roof, where a view of the city is captured. Note the lake at the foot of the mountains.

A view of the Three Pagodas, the big man-made attraction here, is also spotted from the hotel roof. We ride bikes by them but don't feel compelled to see more. The fresh air and scenery are so much more interesting. The weather is perfect.

The Foreigners Are in 709

We see this several times on this trip—
people handwashing their clothing in the street

We love the trendy, bohemian restaurants here. This is Jack's Place, where we treat ourselves to several over-the-top Western breakfasts. Ella's enjoying her fancy beverage and breakfast.

This seems like such a great idea. I want to go to a market in a neighboring town promising all sorts of treasures. So, wouldn't renting bikes be fun? The girls are apprehensive about riding by themselves. Solution—we rent bicycles built for two. When the owner takes my passport and says the shop closes at 6, I think, "So what? We'll be back in two hours." Six hours later, ten minutes before the shop closes, we return never having made it to the market, flat tire repaired, exhausted, severely sunburned, and vowing never to ride more than two hours on a bike ever again. In fact, ever riding a bike again is in question.

There are some positives to our outing. The terrain is flat and incredibly beautiful with the rice paddies and the lake. We do find a bed and breakfast for lunch—if not for this, we would've been truly miserable because we packed nothing to eat or drink. In fact, we packed NOTHING.

The Foreigners Are in 709

In our defense, we were only going for an hour bike ride to a market where we would BUY things. Too bad we misjudged the distance. Six hours in the hot sun with no one to call to pick us up and no one stopping to give us a ride is depressing. Also, pedaling for two, at times, is just too much. Whose idea was this anyway?

We reward ourselves for our ordeal by going to the restaurant across from the bike shop. It's as far as we can walk. I have the best margarita ever, Rose has the biggest bowl of chocolate ice cream ever, and Jim and Ella slurp down huge fresh fruit drinks. We return to the hotel to lie flat on our beds for as long as possible before finding a store that sells aloe.

This is Hong Long Jing Lu, or Red Dragon Well Street. This extremely picturesque walking street has a stream meandering down the center and kitschy shops and cafés lining the sides. Jim and Ella set up camp here sipping fresh lemonades while Rose and I shop.

This is so Chinese. Again, this Chinese family is getting right in the middle of the setting regardless of the perils or appropriateness. It does make for a great picture.

Jim practices his Chinese with anyone who will listen. Here he is with the Monkey King. The Monkey King's sidekick, the pig, scampers off. These things scare me. Jim scares them.

There are five restaurants in a row displaying bountiful still lifes of veggies on terraced platforms.

Eels, bull frogs, and some other critters are at the base. Not as appetizing as the veggies to me, but very interesting and ... fresh.

The Foreigners Are in 709

The subtle focal point of this picture is supposed to be the women carrying the loads of brick and building debris on their backs in the brown baskets. The building next to the restaurant we're sitting at is being torn down, and these women are doing the hard labor. In this region, there is a minority, the Naxis, in which the women do all the work. The men play chess and checkers and don't contribute in any substantial way to their communities until after age forty. Know any Naxis in the U.S.?

As mentioned, the two-hour train ride to Lijiang is fully booked, so we buy bus tickets for the three-and-a half-hour bus ride, which is scheduled to leave at 8:30 that evening. However, at 5:30 all the passengers are at the bus station, so they load us up and we leave. We arrive in Lijiang at 9:00 p.m., even after stopping at a rest stop. On the ride, I get to sit in the front next to the driver. It's one of the scariest experiences of my entire life. It's a mountainous drive with lots of curves, and our driver likes to pass on the curves if at all possible. The scenery is amazing though. These pictures are taken from the bus window. We see corn fields, terraced rice paddies, crops I don't recognize, herds of black goats, cows, pigs, chickens, wind turbines, mountains, and people along the way. Many of the livestock and people are walking in the road, as we swerve past them.

These little red trucks are everywhere and drive well below the speed limit. We pass them all regardless of oncoming traffic.

Sun setting over the rice paddies

Now, having survived the bus ride, we're in Lijiang. We stay at the Dongba Hotel, which is listed in *Lonely Planet*, and I highly recommend it. We stay two nights in two different rooms. This is our bedroom the first night. The girls sleep downstairs.

This is the one-hundred-year-old turtle that lives at our hotel. I'm not sure how they know his age but that's their story.

Now, I'm going to share pictures of the sights we see because the pictures show how beautiful this town is. There's not a lot I can add.

Our view of the street scene from a second-floor restaurant. The town is very touristy, but the weather is gorgeous, and everything is so bright and colorful.

Another view from the restaurant

I think this is the cutest puppy ever. The staff at our hotel is not so enthralled and calls him "the dog that pees everywhere." I find this to be cute. It's funny how your perspective changes when it's not your stuff or your responsibility.

This contraption reminds me of something from Charlie and the Chocolate Factory. Unfortunately, the wild walnut cake tastes pretty bad.

Ella and Jim on separate sofa swings. Our room is behind Jim on the first floor.

Family photo outside the entrance to our hotel

Rose in front of a shop

Restoration of the old town is ongoing. The craftsmanship is incredible.

Do you know what the medallions are? Tea, of course—you're in China. The tea is compressed into molds to form the shape. In ancient China, they used them to make the beverage tea or they could be eaten. They were also used as currency.

And this is a tea shop.

We've made it back to Kunming and are waiting for our plane to Beijing. Apparently, yak meat is a big deal in Yunnan. Jim buys some packaged yak to give to Jenny and Simon. The last gift I brought back from our travels they inadvertently returned to us, and it was too awkward for me to return it to them. So, this time, we hope Jenny and Simon don't give the yak back or that it doesn't cause a heart attack. We yakked a lot about the yak on our way back while it was in our sack and wondered how it would taste on a Big Mac. Watch out, Dr. Seuss.

Making Our Way Back to America

Unwanted Staycation

I'm so mad and frustrated that I don't know what to do. One short, nondescript, unimpressive man has the power to detain us and does. It's July 1, my birthday, and my husband has promised me that "no matter what, we will be back in the USA on your birthday"—remember, you gain a day going home.

Initially, we were to leave China on December 28, 2012. Then, we rebooked our tickets for June 5, 2013—one year from our arrival date. Then, we're supposed to have guests, and we rebook for July 1 with the promise I will finally be home on the first, no later…. No matter what. Remember, Jim already got to spend three months at home during tax season.

I've been a real trooper. While my husband has complained about being bored the last few months, I've continued with my jobs, found new places to explore, and made the most of where we are but now, I'm ready to be home. We have a lot to look forward to. A class party is being thrown for Rose by one of her classmates. I'm to celebrate my birthday with friends. We have two weeks to re-immerse ourselves before being on a schedule again, and we will be back in our own home, in our own comfortable beds with our own things. I'm so ready that I can't stand it.

For the past several weeks, we have been preparing to leave. The Chinese have a custom of taking friends who are

The Foreigners Are in 709

making big trips to dinner and gifting them with very nice presents before they leave. Some do this in the U.S., but in China, everyone we become well acquainted with does this for us—Jenny and Simon, Wan, Sufang and Thomas, my school colleagues, Nea, and Cassie have all fed and gifted us. We've given away all our household goods; we have paid our bills, given up our apartment and unenrolled the girls from school. Jim has taken TaoTao to be examined, and she has her papers, medication, and airline-approved carrier. I have purchased gifts for friends and have packed our bags to the limit, each weighing no more than fifty pounds, which means things have been rearranged several times to the point of not knowing whose belongings are where.

Elaborate arrangements have been made to transport us to the airport. This includes our family of four, TaoTao, our luggage, Daniel, and Jenny. Daniel will be flying home with us and staying for five weeks. Jenny hired an SUV and a taxi for the hour-plus ride to the airport.

We get a heads-up the week before from Wan, our landlord. He says the police called him about our visas being overstayed. I'm sure this isn't going to be a problem because when we came back from Japan and checked in at the neighborhood police station, the policeman said all we needed to do was check in again in thirty days and he would give us another residence slip. This policeman spoke good English, and I wrote down his name and badge number as proof.

After talking with Wan, Jim checks online to see whom we need to talk with. I had spoken to Sufang a month ago about this, and she had given me some written information. Jim didn't think we needed to do anything at that point. Now, he becomes concerned. So, the next day we head to the Entry Exit Bureau, which I thought would be in some remote part of the city accessed only by taxi. Come to find out, it's in the area I've been touring for the last two months. It's almost next to the Lama Temple.

What we find out is that the girls and I have overstayed our visas by almost thirty days. The neighborhood policeman was totally wrong. At Entry Exit, we're also told it will take five days to get new visas, but since our flight leaves in three, we should just take the maximum fine amount— $2,000—to the airport on the day of our flight. We're still very hopeful we'll be home on July 1. I can't imagine not leaving.

What we don't know is that new Chinese immigration laws take effect on July 1. So, here we are at the airport, we have checked in, our bags have been checked, and we head to immigration. Jim and Daniel go first with no problem. The girls and I are next. There's a problem. I show them the note from the police officer and we explain that we've been to Entry Exit and they say all we need to do is pay the fine.

The conversation with the immigration officer is like ping pong:
"No, you have no valid visa and must go to Entry Exit to obtain one."
"We have money to pay the fine."
"No, you've overstayed your visa by many days, and this is not possible."
"This is just one thirty-day interval we overstayed, and we have obeyed the thirty-day requirement for the past year."

"No, you have overstayed a very long time."
"We were told we could extend our visa for thirty days with no problem. The neighborhood police officer told us this would not be a problem."
"No, the laws changed today, and you don't have a valid visa."
"Can we see a supervisor?"
"No."

I am so mad that I ask if he has a gun. "No." "Good, because I would like to shoot you. I follow this by sarcastically saying, "You are the nicest, most understanding person in the world, and I would like to shoot you." Jim, horrified, tries to reason with him that it's my birthday and couldn't he make an exception? "No." And then the man has the nerve to say, as we're walking away with our two adopted Chinese daughters, a Chinese boy who we're opening our home to, and an ill-tempered Chinese cat, that we should have gifted him with, "Happy birthday." Should he not have been shot?

I will accept minimal blame for this situation. Jim had investigated extending the visas months ago and was the one who informed me that there was a way to extend them for the last visa period without leaving China. I left this totally up to him. But during my interrogation at Entry Exit, I have to sign papers admitting MY guilt and stating that "I made my children overstay their visas and I must receive punishment because of this." I sign the papers, which take them two days to process, we pay the fine, and then we apply for the visas. It now takes seven days to get a visa, not including weekends.

Our fine is just the tip of the iceberg of our "punishment." After staying in The Crown Plaza hotel because I want the comforts of home, eating all meals out and rebooking our flights, including Daniel's, we spend about $7,000 in the fifteen days it takes us to get our visas and get on another flight home. What a waste.

I'm so undone by all of this. I wear the same outfit for the next several days and spend much of our staycation reading the Western newspapers in the Western-style lobby of The Crown Plaza trying to ignore the situation. I don't want to hear Chinese or eat anything Chinese because I'm pretending I'm not in China.

Yes, it's childish, but this is how I choose to deal with the situation and it does make me feel a little better. I consider a continuous state of inebriation, but I'm not a drinker and I think I would have felt worse. The kids and Jim keep their distance.

Jim makes arrangements with Cassie to organize a day camp for the girls during our last unexpected week. This includes going to some Chinese homes that have children our children's ages. The kids complain, but it gives them something to do and we get a break from each other.

What makes all this worse is that our homecoming is canceled. Rose's party is canceled. My birthday isn't celebrated, and we come back to a harried schedule. Oh, we are also supposed to host my principal from Vanthink while she visits Rose and Ella's American school for the possibility of an exchange program between the schools. All of that must be rearranged. We miss so much, and after being gone for over a year, our homecoming is a non-event.

So, lesson learned—never let your visa expire. It's a big deal. And, if you really want to go home, the fine is only the beginning of the misery.

One day during our staycation, we eat lunch at Subway and by happenstance sit with a family from Atlanta. I tell them our story, and the husband relays his experience in England, where he had overstayed his visa by two days. He was interrogated by the police in a small room with a bright lightbulb. It was very intense.

In comparison, my interview was nothing. Two very innocent-looking, twenty-year-old female officers asked me questions from a form, but mainly they wanted to talk about the Disney princesses. Thank God I have young children and am well versed.

It's more than a year later, and it's taken me this long to write about this experience. Not being able to go home when we had planned was unbelievably frustrating and almost unbearable for me. I had a very hard time reconciling the fact that I couldn't get home and had little control over the situation.

My bad feelings had little to do with China but everything to do with wanting to be home and dealing with the frustration of not being able to get there. I don't think it matters so much where you are. We were once stranded in Paris because of wind shear. It doesn't get much better than Paris, but I couldn't wait to leave. When I want to go home, there's a tunnel vision that takes over and nothing will do but to be home. There's no place like home.

Even though our last two weeks in China weren't the happiest—in fact, I was truly miserable— it was part of the adventure. Our overall experience was better than we could have ever imagined. Would we do it again? Yes, in a heartbeat.

Coming Home

My cousin, who lives overseas, warned me that we might lose friends upon reentry. She said some people won't be interested in our year in China and how it's changed us. This added to my churning anxiety. I'd worked myself up a bit about coming home. I was feeling nervous about fitting back in and the whole reverse culture shock phenomenon I experienced as an exchange student only compounded my fears.

Now, as we settle back in, I find that most of the people we know are genuinely interested in our experience. I try to be conscious not to go on and on about "when we were in China this" and "when we were in China that." Nobody likes that. So, on the friends' front, I think we're fine.

I do wonder if we've changed. Have we changed? As I write, I see that some of my perspectives on my life and on America are a little different ….

To be honest, the first few months I'm flooded with varying emotions. Tears come very easily. At the Charlotte airport, we needed to call our friends who'd volunteered to give us a ride home. Our cell phones didn't work in the U.S., so I went to the lost-and-found in the baggage claim area to ask to use a phone. There was the friendliest clerk in there, "Yes, help yourself to the phone." He was helping another person and just gabbing, which I joined into. It was so nice to be home, in the South, where people can make you feel so at home. It was also nice to know every single thing that was happening around me. I understood every word, the body language, every sound, every nuance—something that hadn't happened in over a year. My eyes welled up and I sniffled as I thanked him.

So, we finally arrive at our house on July 15, 2013. We don't have the gradual "being back" cushion we planned. We arrive home and hit the ground running.

We not only have our two daughters, but we've also invited our Chinese friends' fifteen-year-old son, Daniel, to spend five weeks with us, which becomes three because of our delay. So, instead of having two weeks to relax and get organized, Daniel and our girls are in day camp the next morning after arriving home at 10:30 p.m. Monday and enduring twenty-two hours of travel.

Daniel is to make a 3-D printer at this week's camp. If he misses another day, he won't be able to catch up and we'll forfeit the almost $1,000 camp fee. And, if Daniel has to go to camp, so do Rose and Ella. I've got things I need to do, and it's just easier not to have the kids around telling me how bored they are.

So, I'm at home trying to catch up on a year's worth of things that I can't postpone any longer. I can no longer say I'm in China and will get to it later. I'm immediately hit with frustration. After being away for a whole year, there's a lot of the same old stuff when we come back. Frankly, it's as if we never left. Things that were either more interesting while we were away or less a part of our lives, like hauling the kids around constantly to activities, the mail (we got one piece of mail in China), paying bills, putting meals on the table, having household and car things fixed, and general obligations—grind on. It's the grind I escaped, and I don't like having it back.

During Daniel's stay, the weight of the grind is alleviated intermittently. This is Daniel's first trip outside China, and we want him to see as much as possible. So, when the kids aren't in camp, we play tourist with him, showing him Charlotte and Americana. We go to a baseball game, take him out for a fancy dinner, tour the Charlotte Motor Speedway, etc. And, because his flight home is from D.C., we show him a good bit of Virginia and our nation's capital—all this in three weeks.

Daniel will go home with the 3-D printer he made, a new basketball from the next week's camp, an ice cream maker his mother wanted, $1,000 worth of American branded clothing and, we hope, a desire to come back. He'll report to mandatory Chinese military training camp his first day back in China. If nothing else, that should solidify his desire.

Touring and entertaining Daniel is a forced and frenzied way to get reacquainted with our country. As we drive Daniel and our girls from activity to activity, I keep thinking what a beautiful city Charlotte is. We live close to

The Foreigners Are in 709

downtown, and I wonder if having the Democratic National Convention earlier in the year plays a part in the beauty I see, or if I just overlooked it in the past. I decide it's probably a little of both.

I notice the big, beautiful, blue skies day after day. The air is light and free of particulates. I notice color and realize Beijing was very gray. Charlotte's buildings gleam; Beijing was covered in a gray grime. The city streets and sidewalks here are colored with healthy blooming plants. We have houses with green lawns and landscapes. In Beijing, our part of the city was all apartments. Plants were "planted" periodically along the streets still in their containers, which I found amusing and puzzling. This worked OK for a couple of days, and then the plants started to die for lack of care.

I see only real cars on well paved roads—no more three-wheeled tin-can cars and motorized wheelchairs intermingled in traffic. A new grocery store, two new apartment buildings, a restaurant and a park have been built in our part of town in the year we were gone. This is a thriving city. Everything looks so well kept … so clean.

As we ride the train from Charlotte to Charlottesville, Virginia, the countryside appears incredibly idyllic, with well-maintained farms with beautiful fences and fields of green grass. It's so green, not brown and scrubby like the countryside I saw many times from the train windows in China.

In Charlottesville, with my sister, Eve, we tour James and Dolly Madison's home and then visit Hot Springs, Virginia, where I grew up. We stay at The Homestead Hotel and coincidentally, get to stay in the James and Dolly Madison Presidential Suite—thanks to connections. Everything from the colonial period to modern day, manmade to natural, looks good from my fresh eyes.

We have a homecoming dinner with my cousins and aunt that my sister-in-law hosts at my childhood home. While I'm visiting with family, the girls, and some cousins are showing Daniel the great outdoors. Daniel has seen deer, butterflies, and horses, which he marvels at intently. He's like a small child interacting with them. We inform him that the deer are wild, and he won't be able to pet them. He gets a dose of reality when one of the horses steps on his foot. He's just never been around animals enough to know it can be dangerous!

As I sit in the bath tub in the enormous, immaculate bathroom of this historic hotel, I cry. Yes, I'm home, where some people still know me. There's something about spending the growing-up years together that bonds you, and when you come home again, your relatives, schoolmates, teachers, and everyone you once knew who's still alive, is truly glad to see you. I'm overwhelmed by this and by the relief of just being home. As I said, the first few months are filled with varying emotions.

From Hot Springs, we drive to D.C. Washington, D.C., is impressive with all its iconic symbols of America. We happen to be there in early August, with unbelievably great weather for touring the Mall area. I'm a very proud American showing off my country. America is even better than I remember.

The Foreigners Are in 709

However, friends are warning me that America is on the brink of exploding. They say our government is gridlocked; guns are out of control, and so on. I can't help but smirk and think to myself, *You don't know how good we have it.*

I love that people are openly complaining. You can't do a lot of that in China. I love that people are angry and are demanding that things be different. The Chinese have been so beaten down by so many years of torture, starvation, and war so recently that many seem afraid and respectfully accept injustices instead of fighting for change.

That's what I've come to love about Americans—we yell and fight and believe we deserve better. That's what will keep America great. I'm now an American bursting with pride…. What a great country.

Afterword

Hindsight

I'm a bit of a worrier where our girls are concerned. Did taking them to China stress them too much? Did losing a year of school harm them academically? Was the trip worth the inconveniences and stress? The jury is still out... But as we now look back on our trip, there are a few things that really stand out and make the whole year seem worthwhile.

For Jim, it was hearing Ella and Rose's classmates yelling to them "Yun Jie," "Qing Cong" after school. The sound of the Chinese children calling our children by their given Chinese names signified to us that our Chinese-American children had become part of the Chinese schoolyard pack. They integrated.

For me, there are two turning points with our girls. Sometime in February or March 2013, Rose and I were together, and she turned to me and said, "You know Mom, people used to scare me, and I didn't want to talk, but now, they don't scare me anymore." Do you know how huge this is? This is the child we packed lunch for all through kindergarten because she was afraid to ask the lunch ladies for the food she wanted.

I believe our China experience and travels really helped Rose come out of her shell. Because I couldn't speak the language and sometimes it was just me and Rose, she had to speak up to get us where we wanted to go or to purchase what we wanted. She did it.

For Ella, the stand-out event was a letter she wrote all in Mandarin to a Chinese friend of ours, Yan Ling. Yan Ling called and told me she couldn't believe how well written the letter was. When we arrived back in Charlotte and had our first parent-teacher conference, Ella's Chinese teacher said her oral Chinese was perfect and her writing was very advanced. That's what a year abroad can do.

When Jim left for three months, I really had to rely on the girls, and they became incredibly mature and responsible in many situations. I believe all the traveling we did also helped. I believe their confidence in themselves grew as they learned they could navigate all the new places and situations we encountered.

Jim learned that no matter how different people seem, we all want the same things. Our friendship with Jenny and Simon gave him insight into a family that works hard and wants the same things as we do for our children. We all have the same hopes and dreams.

For me, China challenged me. I did so many things outside my comfort zone and loved the feeling of being stretched and being more than I was. It makes me continue to venture out of myself and look for what I want to do, not just what I think I can do.

So … travel is good. Everyone should do it. Here's to the next adventure—ours and yours.

Travel Tips

- Always count your baggage whenever you move it—changing hotel rooms, getting on/off planes, trains, taxis, subways, etc.
- Pack light—five tops, five bottoms, pajamas, toiletries, a pair of sneakers, a pair of sandals, and as much underwear as wanted. One small stuffed animal and a "blankie" also make the cut, along with all prescribed and recommended medicines. Wear comfortable, warm clothes on the plane.
- Get a prescription sleeping pill for the long flights and train rides. Try it several times at home first.
- Have a positive trip motto.
- Get your laundry done in Hong Kong by the pound. Don't wait until China, where they charge per piece.
- Get a business card or something from the hotel with its name and address on it.
- Cross the street when the natives cross.
- Designate a person to be the passport holder. This person always gathers the passports after going through security or whenever the passports are dispersed.
- Look for the wonderful food courts in the basement of Chinese mega malls.
- On bus trips, take a picture of your bus and, if possible, your bus driver. Believe me, it's hard to remember which one's yours, especially in a parking lot with row upon row of buses.
- Always take the taxi receipt. You never intend to leave anything behind, but it does happen. Also, taxi drivers sometimes omit items.

- Don't drink water from the faucet in China. You must boil it first.
- Use a small bank in the U.S. where you can talk to an actual person you know, like, and trust.
- Bank of China is the best bank for foreigners because their money transfers are said to be the easiest.
- When transferring money into China, you must go to your Chinese bank to exchange the currency into Chinese RMB before the balance will appear in your Chinese ATM account.
- If a restaurant is crowded, it's probably good.
- If you end up with a standing ticket on a train, get on either the first or last car and look for vacant seats. There's usually more room in these cars.
- Book your reservations on a Chinese website in Chinese, if possible. You'll get the best price.
- Just because you get to a place first, it doesn't mean you'll get in first. The Chinese don't line up for many things, but Koreans and Japanese do.
- Taking a bus into town from the airport gives you a good sense of the city you're visiting, as opposed to taking the subway.
- If you're going to stay in a hostel, Japan is a good place to do it. We find they're clean and well run.
- If you plan to visit the Great Wall, prepare yourself for a hike. I recommend going to Mutianyu.
- Visit the parks in China. They give a real insight into the culture.
- Pay close attention to your visa requirements and obey them.

Acknowledgments

I'd like to thank all the people mentioned in this book who made the planning of our trip easier, who made it possible by taking on some of our responsibilities, and who joined us or whom we met that made our experiences richer.

Those not mentioned who need a big thank you include: Ron Heath, who managed our rental properties and said, "Don't worry about anything. I'll take care of it," and did; my sisters, Deborah and Eve, who did my workload for our family business; Lee Molina, who is the greatest organizer on Earth and packed most of our household; Zoe and Claudia who cared for our cars; and David Hutchinson who took care of the business and loose ends.

I'd like to thank all the people in my life who have nourished my soul and encouraged me. This includes my book club, especially Melva Hannah, who read my blog while we were in China and told me my blog could be a book after a "writer" told me it didn't work; my lunch buddy, Sara Vavra, who also read the blog, helped me set goals, and held me somewhat accountable; my monthly girls lunch group for always being supportive; and Robbi Meador Walls who was the first to read the book and assured me it's a fun, interesting read and helped me make it better.

Thank you to those who helped me write the book. To Liz Hatley, who suggested I take a writing class from Maureen Ryan Griffin; Maureen, who guided me through the whole process from writing class to editing to publishing; Colin

Cooler, who introduced me to organizational and layout ideas; Beth Thompson, who was my final editor and supportive friend; Annie Standish, who clarified the publishing process; and Karel Lucander who shared marketing ideas. Also, of course, a huge hug to Ella who created the front cover and Jody Mayers who tweaked it.

I also need to acknowledge my sources. The maps are from the CIA website The World Factbook. The Beijing guidebooks I used are *Travel in Beijing,* compiled by Deng Changyou and Yang Shuqun, and *Revised and Updated China Beijing English Tour Guiding in Beijing 2011.*

Extra special thanks go to Page Massie and Glenn Nash for their friendship and all their help from adopting Valentino, phone conversations while we were in China, and welcoming us back to the final steps of wardrobe, makeup, and photos for the book cover.

www.ingramcontent.com/pod-product-compliance
Lightning Source LLC
LaVergne TN
LVHW051037080426
835508LV00019B/1573